My Hero Hurts!!

A Study Guide for Teenagers Whose Parents May Have Combat Trauma

Written by Sherry Barron
Illustrated by Nick Adducci

Published by Cru Military, a division of Campus Crusade for Christ, Inc., P.O. Box 120124, Newport News, VA 23612, USA. For more information about Cru Military, please visit our web site at www.crumilitary.org or call 1-757-928-7200 or toll-free in the USA, 1-800-444-6006.

All Scripture quotations unless noted otherwise are taken from the Holy Bible, English Standard Version Copyright © 2001 by Crossway Bibles, a publishing ministry of Good News Publishers.

Chapter Six quotes are from the "Have You Heard of the Four Spiritual Laws?" booklet written by Bill Bright. Copyright 1965, 1994. New Life Publications, a ministry of Cru, formerly known as Campus Crusade for Christ.

Chapter Seven quotes from the "Have You Made the Wonderful Discovery of the Spirit-Filled Life?" booklet written by Bill Bright. Copyright 1966, 1995. New Life Publications, a ministry of Cru formerly known as Campus Crusade for Christ.

Chapter Seven quotes from the "How You Can Walk in the Spirit" Transferable Concept booklet written by Bill Bright. Copyright September 2010. New Life Resources, a ministry of Cru, formerly known as Campus Crusade for Christ.

Illustrations by Nick Adducci

ISBN: 978-0-9863630-2-3

Printed in the United States of America

DISCLAIMER

This book is not a substitute for appropriate medical or psychological care for those experiencing significant emotional pain or whose ability to function at home, school or work is impaired. Chronic or extreme stress may cause a wide assortment of physical and psychological problems. Some may require evaluation and treatment by medical or mental health professionals. When in doubt, seek advice from a professional.

Table of Contents

Dear Readers,

Welcome to a great resource giving teenagers answers to family situations involving a parent or loved one exhibiting symptoms of Post-Traumatic Stress Disorder (PTSD) or Traumatic Brain Injury (TBI). The injuries from serving in a war zone could be physical but also emotional. This book is written with the dad being the one with Combat Trauma but could easily be adapted if another family member is dealing with it.

The study guide aids small group leaders in taking teens through a discussion time of learning and speaking in a small group setting. It can also be used for teens coming alongside teens as a foundational piece for a better understanding of why things are different. The book can be used on an individual basis if a small group gathering is not possible.

We hope the benefits of discussing, informing, praying and supporting teens while a parent or loved one heals will be spread throughout the whole family structure. Our aim is to put a book in the hands of teens which gives solid answers to critical questions and leads to understanding concerning PTSD/TBI and what part God plays in a brighter future for the whole family.

Warmly,

Sherry Barron

Sherry Barron and the Cru Military staff team

Dear Small Group Leader,

Congratulations, small group leader, on deciding to use this resource to help teens through the journey of coping with Combat Trauma. Teens experiencing a life at home, which is not as it used to be, will be encouraged to know they don't have to go through it alone. The Cru Military staff and volunteers want to encourage you to use this guide in helping teens learn about and discuss the issues related to Post-Traumatic Stress Disorder (PTSD) or Combat Trauma which one or more of their loved ones may be experiencing. Many military families affected by Combat Trauma are not getting the help they need. Their children are often confused and have unanswered questions.

The focus of this study guide is to give teens some answers to many of their questions. It is also created to bring teens together and help them encourage each other in the group as they think through, talk about and see God at work. The Cru Military staff wants teens and their families to seek a relationship with Jesus Christ as part of the healing process for themselves and the ones in their families who are suffering with Combat Trauma. Healing is achieved because God gives His guidance, comfort, love, peace and joy in the midst of the journey for each member of the family.

Many of the **"What to Ask?"** questions are designed for group members to draw from their personal opinions and experiences. If you as a leader share any of these points from your own life, be sure to do so in a manner that does not stifle discussion by making you the authority with the final answers. Begin your comments by saying things like, "One thing I notice in this passage is ..." or "I think another reason for this is ..." Each of the families depicted in this study guide are not real families but the writing depicts real-life scenarios that could happen as a result of Combat Trauma.

Be mindful that the sharing in the group sessions:

- should not embarrass any member of the family or other students.
- should not force everyone to give an answer to every question.
- should only stay in the group and not be told to anyone else. (The exception would be when finding out about any abuse, danger or information that should be shared with authorities.)
- should include a lot of positive encouragement.

May God bless you on your journey of guiding teens through Combat Trauma issues!

Foreword

Chances are you're holding this book and reading this forward because someone you love very much went to war and came home a different person. You also are feeling the effect of Combat Trauma.

Cru Military's "Bridges to Healing" project first focused on providing Christ-centered solutions for warriors coming home with spiritual wounds of Combat Trauma and Post-Traumatic Stress Disorder (PTSD). Author Chris Adsit wrote **The Combat Trauma Healing Manual** providing Biblical answers to address these wounds. Soon, realizing Combat Trauma affects the whole family and that wives face unique challenges, Chris Adsit, Rahnella Adsit and Marshéle Carter Waddell wrote **When War Comes Home**, providing factual information about Combat Trauma and PTSD. Its 13 chapters lead wives on a journey of healing for secondary trauma stress.

"Please get me something to help the children. They're getting lost." This was the cry of military chaplains from all branches when Cru Military asked, "How can we help you?"

With a passion to help military children, Sherry Barron used her experience as a military wife, mother, educator and author to write this book, **"My Hero Hurts!! A Guide for Teenagers Whose Parents May Have Combat Trauma."**

Following the 13-chapter format of *When War Comes Home*, this series of children's books also includes **My Hero's Home!!** (K-3 Grade) and **Helping My Hero!!** (4-6 Grade). The Christ-centered solutions and unique formats in these books will help communication between parents and their children.

In addressing the effects of Combat Trauma on children, this book fulfills a vision we've had since the Vietnam War. We saw these effects firsthand while in the Army, as Cub Scout leaders and while teaching in the Department of Defense School in Schweinfurt, Germany. As we studied the stresses on our military families serving during the Afghanistan and Iraq wars, the vision became clear. We are very appreciative of Cru Military, their financial supporters and Sherry Barron for making this vision a reality. We pray you receive spiritual healing from the Christ-centered solutions in this book.

Ron and Marcy Wheat
Cru Military Missionaries

Chapter 1

What happened to Dad?

Understanding

Meet the Williams family. Troy is a high school senior and the oldest of the three children, A lot is expected of him, especially when his father is away for months on end. Troy's family has led the military lifestyle as long as he has been alive. Because he is a great student and a natural leader, his mom depends on him to help with getting his siblings where they have to be most days of the week. His younger teenage sister, Misty, and brother, Joel, admire and look up to him. They are expecting their dad home soon from his fifth deployment in seven years. The family is working their way through a checklist they devised after the second deployment to make the homecoming an easy transition. *(See their list in the Appendix on page 126.)*

Troy's mom has secretly felt there was something going on with her husband's personality because their communication with one another has been different from the previous deployments. She was looking forward to seeing her husband face to face so she could look him in the eyes to see what's going on. As the family thoroughly cleaned up their home and the garage, and made the yard look very trim and neat, they were getting more excited to have their dad home again. Little did they know it was not going to ever be the same.

The day finally arrived and the Williams family members were poised to catch a glimpse of their loved one climb off the bus which transported the returning Marines to the base. They had been waiting hours for just the right bus but when they saw that one special Marine hit the ground, they shouted, "Hey, Dad, over here!" Captain Williams waved and pointed towards the area where all the duffel bags and equipment were laid out on the tarmac. It seemed like chaos as all the cami-uniformed Marines were wandering through the endless rows in search of the bags marked with their names. Friends would shout out to each other if they located a set of bags for their fellow Marines. Finally, Bill Williams joined his family, ready for the long hugs and kisses all around.

Several months passed by and life appeared to be getting back to normal. After the family had enjoyed a short leave time hiking, fishing and relaxing at a friend's nearby lake-front cottage, the transition from 'no dad' to 'dad being home' seemed to have gone smoothly. But Captain Williams didn't talk about his combat experiences with anyone in the family, so no one knew what was happening inside his head and heart.

Finally Troy, Misty and Joel asked their mom what had happened to the dad they used to have, because he was not the same father they knew. Everyone sensed something was not quite right and it seemed to be getting worse as time passed by. Increasingly the kids felt like they had to be so careful to not make loud noises, or shout, or get their dad angry. He would get so irritated about little stuff. When he asked the kids to do something around the house and they procrastinated, he became livid. He seemed to be overreacting most of the time.

They didn't know that their dad's unit had experienced some fierce fighting in this last deployment and many of his men had been seriously injured and several had died violent deaths.

What to learn?

Note: The Williams family has heard about Post-Traumatic Stress Disorder (PTSD) in the news but it never occurred to them that their father was suffering with this affliction. The change in behavior didn't seem to be going away, and family life as they had known it before had changed. There are many who have returned recently from the battles of war with symptoms that go untreated. It is time to get informed with the issues involving PTSD.

What can cause the wounds of war?

1. Traumatic combat-related events happening all around them

2. Tension from being constantly on alert because of Improvised Explosive Devices (IEDs) concealed along the roadways

3. Suspicious vehicles that could explode at any time

4. Being affected by threats, trauma, pain, atrocity, horror and gore

5. Facing death 24/7

6. Physical, emotional, psychological and soul wounds from the trauma

What causes PTSD?

- Being involved in any horrific event such as combat, sexual and physical assault, being held hostage, terrorism, torture, natural and man-made disasters, accidents, or receiving a diagnosis of a life-threatening illness

- Witnessing threatening behavior, hearing about a close family member or friend living through a life-threatening experience or knowing that someone intentionally caused the trauma

What happens to the whole body because of trauma?

- Adrenaline and noradrenalin hormones are dumped into the bloodstream.

- The heart beats faster.

- The lungs pump harder.

- The body gets ready to either fight, fly or freeze.

- The pupils in the eyes dilate giving a person tunnel vision.

- Thousands of small muscles in the arms and legs constrict.

- Blood is drawn away from the skin and into the muscles for quick movement, if needed.

- The blood sugar and free fatty acids instantly ramp up giving more energy.

- Up to 70% of the brain-bound oxygen is quickly shunted into the muscles.

- Additional hormones give uncommon strength and quickness.

- Right-brain alarms go off and drown out the logical analysis of the left brain.

- The lower brain takes over and directs the rest of the body to stay focused and survive.

What are the symptoms of PTSD?

Note: Check any notable behaviors you have seen or heard spoken about from your loved one. Put a check-mark if the behavior was in the past and an X if the behavior is currently happening.

- ☐ Nightmares, night terrors
- ☐ Sleepwalking, sleep-fighting
- ☐ Unwanted images, thoughts, or daydreams
- ☐ Flashbacks (feeling like he's reliving the traumatic event)
- ☐ Fixated on war experience, living in the past
- ☐ Spontaneous psychotic episodes, when the world as he knows it disappears
- ☐ Panic attacks, undefined dread or fear
- ☐ Avoiding anyone or anything that reminds him of the traumatic event
- ☐ Self-isolating, dread of social interaction
- ☐ Anxiety in crowds, traffic
- ☐ Inability to trust others
- ☐ Very reluctant to talk about his traumatic event(s)
- ☐ Lack of interest or motivation regarding work, recreation, former hobbies, or exercises
- ☐ Close relationships are now distant

- ☐ Emotional numbness, flat affect - not happy or sad but "dead" inside
- ☐ Substance abuse to numb himself and escape the moment
- ☐ Suicide attempts
- ☐ Physical fatigue
- ☐ Neglect/abandon personal care, hygiene, nutrition, exercise
- ☐ Anger, easily irritated, "short fuse," fits of rage
- ☐ Hypervigilance or always on guard with a weapon close by
- ☐ Easily startled, reacts to loud noises, jumpy
- ☐ Poor memory
- ☐ Trouble falling asleep or staying asleep, insomnia
- ☐ Night sweats
- ☐ Accelerated heart rate, rapid breathing, heart palpitations for no good reason
- ☐ Abandons or questions faith, feeling betrayed or abandoned by God, mad at God
- ☐ Fear of becoming violent, becoming violent, provoking fights
- ☐ Self-mutilation, cutting, excessive tattooing

What is the difference between PTSD & Traumatic Brain Injury (TBI)?

- TBI is usually the result of a sudden, violent blow to the head.

- The skull can often handle a forceful, external impact without fracturing.

- A blow to the head can launch the brain on an internal collision with the skull.

- An injured brain inside an intact skull is known as a "closed-head injury."

- A brain injury also occurs when a projectile, such as a bullet, rock, or fragment of a fractured skull penetrates the brain.

- Shock wave blasts from IED's, rocket propelled grenades and land mines are the leading cause of TBI for active duty military personnel in a war zone today.

- Reports indicate over 150,000 service members have sustained a TBI injury in the last decade of war in the Middle East.

What are the symptoms of TBI?

- ☐ Headaches
- ☐ Memory problems
- ☐ Ringing in ears
- ☐ Poor word recall
- ☐ Difficulty concentrating
- ☐ Irritability or anger outbursts
- ☐ Lack of forethought
- ☐ Inflexible in thought
- ☐ Depression
- ☐ Negative attitude
- ☐ Antisocial or isolated
- ☐ Poor judgment
- ☐ Change in sexual drive or ability
- ☐ Limited range of affect, restricted in emotions
- ☐ Seizures
- ☐ Slowed or impaired motor skills
- ☐ Speech problems

Note: Check any notable behaviors you have seen or heard spoken about from your loved one. Put a check-mark if the behavior was in the past and an X if the behavior is currently happening. Only a healthcare professional can properly assess the situation but it is good to know what to look for.

- ☐ Loss of sense of taste or smell
- ☐ Avoidance behavior
- ☐ Dizziness or vertigo
- ☐ Balance problems
- ☐ Sleep problems
- ☐ Difficulty reading
- ☐ Visual disturbances
- ☐ Impulsive behavior
- ☐ Obsessive/compulsive
- ☐ Anxiety
- ☐ Sensitivity to light, touch, sound
- ☐ Gets lost or becomes misdirected

What to ask?

Note: Answer the following questions truthfully but remember to be respectful of each other and your family members. Be a good listener. Do not share or repeat anything you hear outside the group. Confidentiality helps make the group a safe place to share from your heart. Everyone should be made to feel accepted no matter what. Everyone should feel open to sharing as this gives hope to those who speak. Sharing God's love and His Word brings encouragement and transformed lives.

 Q.1 Has your family ever experienced what the Williams family started noticing about their dad after a deployment? If so, share your experience with the group.

_____

_____

_____

_____

 Q.2 Has your family life been disrupted by any of the symptoms in either the PTSD group (on page 11) or the TBI group (on page 14)? What unusual behaviors is your loved one displaying?

_____

_____

_____

_____

 Q.3 Has your family sought professional help/spiritual help in dealing with the changes in your family dynamics? If so, what happened?

_____

_____

_____

_____

What to take away?

Five things military teens want to understand

1. *"If 'God so loved the world,' then why is my dad different from when he was deployed the last time?"* Unfortunately, the sinful actions of people cause bad circumstances such as war. History has proven that selfishness, warring factions, conquests and oppression lead to trouble and chaos. The horrors of war can result in killing, maiming and/or emotionally scarring those in battle.

2. God is always present wherever there is conflict but people need to turn to Him for comfort, guidance and assurance that He is with them at all times.

3. God has a plan to eliminate evil and those who practice evil, but in the meantime, military personnel are needed to keep peace as much as possible.

4. *"What should I feel about God right now?"* Put an "X" in the box that best describes your own feelings.

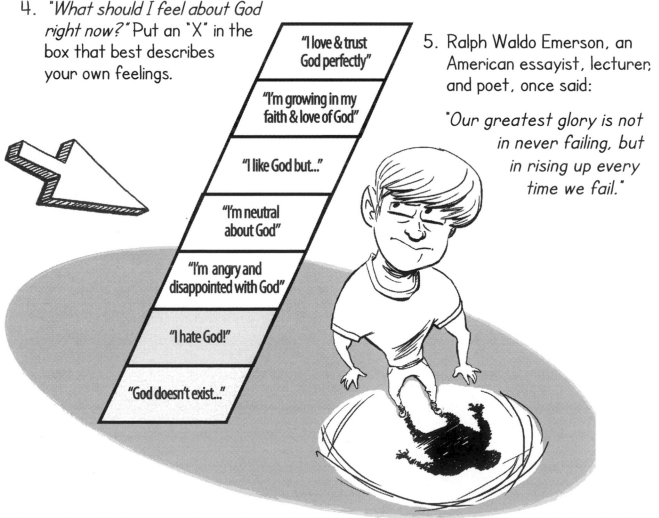

"I love & trust God perfectly"

"I'm growing in my faith & love of God"

"I like God but..."

"I'm neutral about God"

"I'm angry and disappointed with God"

"I hate God!"

"God doesn't exist..."

5. Ralph Waldo Emerson, an American essayist, lecturer, and poet, once said:

   "Our greatest glory is not in never failing, but in rising up every time we fail."

Remember God wants to be totally involved in the healing process for the whole family. He is waiting for each member of the family to count on Him.

What does God say?

2 Timothy 2:7 – *"Think over what I say, for the Lord will give you* **understanding** *in everything."*

Do you believe this is true? Why or why not?

_____

_____

_____

What to pray?

"Lord, our family is just beginning to learn more about PTSD and TBI. We want to know how to help our dad and understand how to support his needs during this time of healing. Help us to trust You for the proper professional input and care. We know You have the power to heal the wounds of the heart. We want to give You this situation and ask for Your guidance as we journey the road together as a family. Help our dad know how much we love him and how much You love him too. Amen"

What's next?

- Keep in mind: Dad's condition is due to the sinful actions of men, not God.

- God wants to be intimately involved in the healing process. Turn to Him.

- Post-Traumatic Stress Disorder is a common reaction to an uncommon event.

- The whole family can be wounded too as a result of living with the one suffering with PTSD/TBI symptoms.

- With God's intervention, your family may experience a stronger lifestyle filled with hope rather than despair and destruction.

Chapter 2

Meet the Garcia family. Victoria and David can't wait for their father to come home from Afghanistan. This year in the new high school is almost over. Victoria is a sophomore and David a freshman. Their mom and dad have been planning a huge family vacation once school was out and Dad was home from his latest deployment. Everyone is looking forward to getting away from all the activities related to school and work. Mrs. Garcia had been a third grade teacher for many years and was so lucky to get a long-term substitute teaching job for the last half of the school year.

Being new to the area and having Sergeant Garcia ship out shortly after the boxes were unpacked had been overwhelming, but everyone seemed to adjust right away. The time has gone by fast because he is due back home any day now. The kids are hoping there would not be a repeat of behaviors in their father that occurred after he came home from his last deployment. Victoria and David had noticed how even though he had seemed thrilled to be back home, he had become quiet and withdrawn. Normally, their father was the life of the party and had lots of friends wherever he served, but he had become like a loner. He would just come home and sit quietly in his room, usually looking at something on the computer.

Even Mrs. Garcia had changed during the two months after the last deployment, but the kids thought it was due to the move to a new base, getting their father ready for the unexpected return back overseas and looking for a teaching job. The kids gradually noticed their mom's spirits lifting after their father left after only being home two months. This seemed strange to them since they were now without their dad again for months on end.

The summer didn't turn out to be what everyone had hoped for. After Sgt. Garcia had returned home and finished the work he had to do before getting leave, the family finally left for the much anticipated camping trip to their favorite national park. They all loved to hike and go mountain biking. The first part of their vacation had all the elements of fun, but not the last few days. When Victoria confronted her mom about a fight she overheard her parents having, her mom burst into tears. She blurted out to her daughter, "Your father is not the same, and I don't know what to do about it."

Mrs. Garcia was in anguish because she saw that her husband was again acting differently towards her, and she was so afraid the children would notice and be affected by the strange behaviors. She saw the questioning look in her daughter's eyes and she wanted everything to be like it was before. Life had been so much sweeter than it is right now. She had thought that the vacation would make a positive difference but it only made things worse. She was so worried about their family's future.

What to learn?

Note: Mrs. Garcia sensed there was a real threat to the well-being of her family's emotional state and wanted to find out all she could to make sure her children were prepared to deal with what lay before them. She felt Victoria and David were old enough to know about the reality of injuries, both physical and emotional, which could appear in people involved in combat action.

What is Secondary Traumatic Stress (STS)?

1. When a person learns what happened to a loved one who has experienced a trauma, and takes on the responsibility of trying to help the suffering person on their own.

2. When a person hears the stories related to the trauma suffered by a loved one and become stressed as a result.

3. When a person receives injuries as a result of violent behavior from a loved one suffering from PTSD/TBI.

What are the symptoms of STS?

Note: Check any notable behaviors you have seen or heard spoken about from your loved one or yourself. Put a check mark if the behavior was in the past and an X if the behavior is currently happening. Only a healthcare professional can properly assess the situation, but it is good to know what to look for.

- ☐ Diminished concentration
- ☐ Forgotten appointments
- ☐ Decreased self-esteem
- ☐ Anxiety
- ☐ Anger, rage, irritability
- ☐ Fearfulness, dread, horror
- ☐ Withdrawn
- ☐ Appetite changes
- ☐ Sadness, depression
- ☐ Compulsiveness (eating, spending)
- ☐ Rapid heartbeat
- ☐ Dizziness
- ☐ Mistrust, suspicious of others
- ☐ Feeling angry at God
- ☐ Feeling God is punishing you

- ☐ Feeling far from God
- ☐ Questioning the meaning of God
- ☐ Confusion, spacey
- ☐ Chronic lateness
- ☐ Nightmares
- ☐ Guilt, shame
- ☐ Survivor guilt
- ☐ Impatience
- ☐ Sleep disturbances
- ☐ Overwhelmed
- ☐ Sweating
- ☐ Aches and pains
- ☐ Feeling unsafe
- ☐ Need to control others
- ☐ Feeling a sense of hopelessness
- ☐ Neglecting prayer, Bible study and fellowship with others

What are three symptoms that bother your loved one or you the most?

1. _____

2. _____

3. _____

What are other symptoms of someone with STS?

Note: Put a check mark by any statement which reveals unusual behavior you have witnessed in a loved one or felt yourself. Use this data when explaining to a professional counselor what is happening as a result of living with someone who has PTSD/TBI.

☐ I find myself avoiding certain activities or situations because they remind me of frightening experiences.

☐ I have gaps in my memory about frightening events.

☐ I feel isolated and estranged from others.

☐ I have outbursts of anger or irritability with little provocation.

☐ I startle easily.

☐ I have thoughts of violence against the people who caused my loved one's trauma.

☐ I have had "flashbacks" about some of the traumatic incidents my loved one shared with me.

☐ I am frightened by things my loved one has said or done to me.

☐ I experience troubling dreams.

☐ I have felt trapped in our family's situation.

☐ I have felt a sense of hopelessness that our family will crumble soon.

☐ I have felt in danger due to the unusual behaviors of my loved one with PTSD/TBI.

☐ I have felt all alone and don't know where to turn for help.

☐ I have a sense of worthlessness because of the way I am being treated by other family members.

☐ I have thoughts that I am a failure as a wife/child in this family.

What are three symptoms that bother your loved one or you the most?

1. _____

2. _____

3. _____

What to ask?

Note: Answer the following questions truthfully but remember to be respectful of each other and your family members. Be a good listener. Do not share or repeat anything you hear outside the group. Confidentiality helps make the group a safe place to share from your heart. Everyone should be made to feel accepted no matter what. Everyone should feel open to sharing as this gives hope to those who speak. Sharing God's love and His Word brings encouragement and transformed lives.

Have you noticed any symptoms, like those in the list starting on page 23, in family members other than the one with PTSD/TBI? How did that make you feel?

_____

_____

_____

_____

_____

Has your family sought the help it needs to assess the behaviors and then get proper treatment for either or both the PTSD /TBI and STS? What were the results?

_____

_____

_____

_____

What is different about your family life as a result of your mom or any of the kids in the family experiencing STS?

_____

_____

_____

_____

What to take away?

Keep the stress from becoming a disorder

Note: God provides a huge advantage to any suffering person who is seeking help and healing from the results of PTSD/TBI/STS. As each element is listed, look up the related verses in the Bible and write in your answers in the space provided. Share with the group what you have discovered as you work on rearranging the stress trigger points in your life.

1. **Be aware of God's love.** It is God who loves unconditionally and desires that all who seek Him, will know Him and realize He is the great healer. Search your heart to see if the turmoil of your family life right now is crowding out the benefits of having a relationship with God. Without having God's son, Jesus Christ, guiding and encouraging you, life can be more difficult for a longer period of time. Look up *John 3:16* and note what it says. What is your action point?

   _____

   _____

   _____

2. **Learn to rest.** It is important to take time to rest while under stress. Physical and emotional stress, whether directly or indirectly causing symptoms, can get tiring and overwhelming. Our bodies are designed to work hard, play hard, fight hard, but then rest in order to restore our bodies, minds and spirits. Make sure your family experiences some kind of rest times so everyone's energies can be restored. Look up *Matthew 11:28* and note what it says. Write one change you can make in your schedule in order to get more rest.

   _____

   _____

   _____

3. **Learn to be silent and learn to be still.** It seems impossible to find any place where there is no noise. Who's got time to be still? Our society wants you to be busy because there is so much to do and see. It is important to intentionally seek to find quiet places and learn more about God and His ways. Look up *Psalm 46* and make note of all the ways God wants to bless those who seek Him and desire to have a relationship with Him.

2

_____

_____

_____

_____

_____

4. **Seek to give your problems to God each day.** Every day, first thing, give all the day's activities to God to handle. You don't have to carry them alone even though you think you can or should. The problems of school life, family life, work life and church life should all be on the list you give God each morning as you start the day. Look up *Matthew 11:29,30* and make note of all that God wants to help you with each day. Write down one or two issues you are going to intentionally give to God to take care of for you.

_____

_____

_____

_____

_____

5. **Learn to prioritize.** It is important for you to figure out what to say 'yes' to and what to say 'no' to. Life is probably coming at you really fast at this time in your life. Remember you don't have to do everything. If it is difficult to fit everything in, prioritize when to do each activity and give yourself grace if it can't all be done today. Be sure to reach the most important goals when they are due. Look up *Philippians 4:19* and make note of how resourceful God is and how He wants to help you with your priorities.

_____

_____

_____

_____

_____

What does God say?

*Psalm 139:1-4 – "O Lord, you have **searched** me and known me! You know when I sit down and when I rise up; you **discern** my thoughts from afar. You **search** out my path and my lying down and are **acquainted** with all my ways. Even before a word is on my tongue, behold, O Lord, you know it altogether."*

Do you believe this is true? _____ Why or why not?

_____

_____

_____

What to pray?

"Lord, help me and my family find the rest we need so we can see healing take place. We love that You are with us and ready at all times to help us with our problems. Help us remember to turn to You for all the things affecting our family and each person in our family. Give us the courage to say 'no' when we should, and not feel guilty. Help everyone seek to know You better, especially those who are hurting the most. Amen"

What's next?

- Find a Prayer Buddy to pray with on a regular basis.

- Be honest with yourself when completing the assessment tools.

- Use angry outbursts as a thermometer to the stresses of life.

- Consider becoming a Battle Buddy for someone.

- Don't be afraid to say to God, "Please hear my cry for help!"

Chapter 3

"Why am I so sad?"

Grieving

Meet the Smith family. Life has definitely changed since hearing the news that Captain Smith had been sent to Germany for treatment of wounds from fighting in Afghanistan. Mary, the oldest teenager in a family of three teens, had been home alone when the call came. When she heard who was calling and that he needed to speak to Mrs. Smith as soon as possible, a pit in her stomach wouldn't go away. She called her mom at work and blurted out there was an emergency call for her.

Mrs. Smith took the news rather well since she and her family have lived the military life for many years. This was the first time her husband had been severely injured and she knew there would be major adjustments for her family to make. But, knowing her great kids, she knew they would do it with flying colors. Even though her oldest son, Steven was only 17, he already knew he wanted to follow in his father's footsteps and join the Marines as soon as he graduated from high school. Mark, their 15-year-old, wanted to go to college and study to be an oceanographer; he loved everything related to what was contained under the ocean water. Mary was enrolled in the local community college taking her prerequisite courses to become a high school English teacher.

The Humvee Captain Smith had been seated in when the blast occurred was the second of several vehicles driving on a narrow road into a village. The driver and soldier in the passenger seat had been killed instantly. The captain was in the back seat was hit by flying shrapnel. One of piece of shrapnel had lodged in his cheek bone just under his right eye. The surgeons were able to save his eyesight but his eye has been covered for weeks. They would be removing the bandages today to see how it's healing. The other points of injury were all healing nicely and the weeks of rehab for his muscles had been going well.

Even though the prognosis seemed positive, there was a sadness his family had not seen in him before. Their father was very quiet these days and didn't engage with them as he had before. Everyone thought it was just part of the healing process and they kept waiting to see him become the man they had known before this last deployment. What they didn't know was Capt. Smith was going through a grieving process affecting his emotions while recovering from his physical wounds. Learning more about the grieving process would help each family member come alongside their father while he healed from pain and loss.

What to learn?

What is grief?

- Grief is always related to some sort of loss.

- Grief is experienced when distress over a loss or affliction is felt.

- Types of loss could include losing car keys, a personal computer crashes, losing family photos to a flooded basement, loss of a favorite pet, loss of a job, loss of a relationship and so much more.

- War zone losses could include losing a buddy in a battle, losing a limb in a bombing, being permanently disabled, losing the ability to function at 100% due to emotional stress, losing a battle to the enemy, survivor's guilt and many other things.

What is the purpose of grief?

- God designed our bodies to process loss to lead us to greater strength, resourcefulness, resilience and faith.

- When we grieve, we are allowing the emotions to be expressed rather than stuffed.

- When we grieve, we are acknowledging injustice and not minimizing it.

- When we grieve, we are facing the loss head on.

- When we grieve, we are not running away or pretending it didn't happen.

What are the symptoms of grief?

Note: Check any symptoms you or your loved one is experiencing. Each person processes grief and loss differently. If many are checked, it could mean grief is being fully felt. If only a few are checked, it could mean there is denial or putting off of the proper way to grieve the loss.

☐ **Fear** of not seeing any improvement in the situation, of harm coming to someone in the family or of the family to never being the same.

☐ **Anger** aimed at the circumstances, at the military, at God for allowing the bad thing to happen or the fact that life will never be the same.

☐ **Rage** may be manifested in yelling, screaming, stomping, slamming doors, kicking the trash can, kicking the dog, throwing things, or more.

☐ **Weeping** - tears at any time, for any reason.

☐ **Guilt** - being consumed with thoughts of "If only I ..." "What if ...?" "I should have ..."

☐ **Loneliness** is the result of people not knowing how to act around those who are grieving; who don't know what to do or say.

☐ **Blaming** - This is so unfair! Where's the justice! What did we do to deserve this? Somebody has to be held accountable! Why didn't the military protect our loved one better? Why doesn't the grieving go away?

☐ **Running away or numbing** is a desperate way to escape. It could be through drugs, alcohol, work, ministry, sex, food, shopping, gambling ... anything to get away from reality.

Other symptoms may include:

☐ Loss of appetite

☐ Overly talkative

☐ Memory lags, mental short-circuits

☐ Unexplained aches and pains

☐ Sleepiness, fatigue, lethargy

☐ Sleeplessness

☐ Nightmares

☐ Feeling abandoned

☐ Frustration

☐ Dehydration

☐ No desire to talk

☐ Feeling out of control

☐ Emotionally overloaded

☐ No feelings at all

☐ Hyperactivity

☐ Others not on this list

3

What are the stages of grief?

Note: Be reminded that each person goes through the stages of grief differently no matter what age. It is normal for anyone to be depressed and sad. Others may not understand and want you to get "over it." A later stage could involve a period of wanting to be isolated and alone so you can deal with everything.
This grief model can help you see that grief is a process,

Stage 1. Shock and Denial

A person may react to learning of a loss with numbed disbelief. Denial that anything has happened is normal in order to avoid the pain of the loss. Shock provides emotional protection to keep from being overwhelmed with all the emotions all at once. It could be weeks before it wears off.

Stage 2. Pain and Guilt

The pain sets in as the shock wears off. Realize the pain should be felt as part of the grieving process. A person may think it is something they said or did that caused the loss. This phase may have unexpectedly chaotic or scary times.

Stage 3. Anger and Bargaining

Frustration at the situation gives way to angry outbursts. Close relationships may be harmed if the anger is not controlled. There could be bargaining episodes which go like this: "I will always keep my room clean, and then Dad can come home."

Stage 4. Depression, Reflection, Loneliness

People close to someone grieving may wonder why it is taking so long for them to heal from their loss. A long period of sad reflection may take over those who are grieving. Often when the reality of the situation sets in, they may isolate themselves on purpose. They want to reflect on things they did with their loved one.

Stage 5. The Upward Turn

As the new way of life settles in, life can become calmer and more organized. The physical symptoms mentioned above may lessen and the depression may begin to fade away.

Stage 6. Rebuild and Work Through

Open communication is key to the family moving forward in a positive way. Getting into a regular routine for all will keep those painful emotions from taking over. Working on projects and problem solving will keep everyone in the family on the right track to healing.

Stage 7. Acceptance and Hope

Life has changed and there will come a time when acceptance of the situation takes place. Acceptance does not necessarily mean complete happiness with no more sadness. When all in the family have come to this stage, hope of a brighter future should come.

What to ask?

 The Smith family experienced grief because of many losses: loss of good health, loss of mission, loss of life as it used to be, etc. Have you ever experienced loss of some kind? What was it, and how did you deal with it?

_____

_____

_____

_____

 Have you seen improvement in the one experiencing grief? What were some of the symptoms, and how has it changed your family dynamics?

_____

_____

_____

 What are some ways you have tried to help the one you have seen exhibiting the grief cycle? Now that you are aware of the steps of grief, have you seen the progress towards acceptance take place?

_____

_____

_____

_____

What to take away?

What is a good way to mourn?

- **Remember where God is in the process.**
  He has a special attraction to anyone who is
  mourning for whatever reason.
- **Remember the past and remain optimistic.**
  Being comforted in the past can sustain
  you through the present loss.
- **Remember to put your faith in the right place.**
  God is right there step by step through the trenches of
  walking the steps through grief; don't rely solely on
  yourself to pull yourself through.
- **Remember you are not alone in your loss.**
  Everyone needs a support group to get
  through the difficult work of grieving.
- **Remember not to bottle up your anger.**
  Bitterness can take over when anger festers and takes
  control...the better plan is to reach out, get help so you
  in turn can help others some day.
- **Remember to write in a journal which
  helps with recovery.**
  Getting your feelings down on paper can
  show how you've moved forward in the
  process of grieving.
- **Remember to change the "why"
  questions to "how" questions.**
  Why did this happen to me? → How can
  I build new dreams?"
  Why did God let this happen? → How can
  I learn from what I have experienced?

What does God say?

*Jeremiah 8:18 – "My joy is gone; **grief** is upon me;*
my heart is sick within me."

Are you or is someone you love experiencing grief? _____
How can God give you comfort at a time like this?

_____
_____
_____
_____

What to pray?

"Lord, You know what our family is experiencing through this turn of events in our lives. You know we are grieving the losses, but You have promised to bless us because we are mourning. Thank You for understanding what each one of us is going through. We desire that You come close to us like never before and pour Your undying love and care into our lives. We want to receive this love more than ever before because we know You have compassion for us. Amen."

What's next?

● Everyone deals with grief differently. Don't compare yourself to anyone else.

● Keep your connection to God open and working. It will give you strength.

● Know that loss leaves a mark on your life, but God will use it positively when the timing is right.

● Be open to the work God is doing and will do in your life as a result of trusting Him with the pain.

Chapter 4

"Why am I so angry?"

Forgiving

Meet the Johnson family. Mitchell and Michael are 16-year-old twins with very different personalities. Having grown up in the military, they have experienced several deployments by both of their parents. In their early years, both their mom and dad served in the military and had gone overseas at different times. Their father, Lt Colonel Johnson, is an orthopedic doctor. Mrs. Johnson had completed her service to the military as an active duty nurse when the twins were 10 years old.

The boys were excellent athletes and played baseball, basketball and football. Their father encouraged them to keep in excellent shape since that was one of the family's values. Everyone in the family ran and worked out almost every day of the week. There didn't seem to be a challenge the family faced that they couldn't overcome.

Mitchell seemed to be taking all of the deployments in stride and was happy to be a part of everything that any military family experiences. Michael, on the other hand, was becoming moodier and was angry about every little thing that did not go his way. The latest episode occurred when he expected his parents to attend the final home football game of the season. At the last minute, his father had to cancel yet again because of an emergency at the hospital. As the star receiver, Michael had helped his team win all season but his father had missed a lot of games.

Michael's bad attitude was often causing angry incidents. His father wasn't taking the time to listen like he did before this latest deployment, but instead would just laid down the law. The twins thought he would get better in time, but their dad had such high expectations for everything, and the boys were feeling the pressure. Mitchell would talk to his mom about what was going on, but Michael began to withdraw from his family, and even his brother, and was spending much more time with his friends. Mitchell was wondering what he'd done wrong. He and Michael used to be so close.

Michael's greatest disappointments were all the broken promises since his dad had come back home. He felt that he'd rather have his father gone than to always feel the pain of disappointment. Sometimes he felt like the military was more important to his dad than his family and that made him mad. He couldn't wait to go away to college and not be disappointed by another broken promise.

What to learn?

4

Note: It appears there are two people in the Johnson family who are hurting more than the others. Because his father had been so focused on finishing his education and then on his service in the military, Michael has built up a pile of resentment from the neglect he has felt. Ever since LTC Johnson returned from the last difficult deployment he's been more distant from his family. Mrs. Johnson was the proactive one in getting everyone to sit down for a family discussion time.

A Family Sit-down Talk Guide

Prior to the scheduled sit-down talk time, each person in the family completed the following questionnaire. *(You will find more questions in the Appendix on page 127.)*

1. What is one thing you really appreciate about each member of your family? Share what you have written down.

    _____

    _____

    _____

2. What is one thing you wish other members of your family understood about you? Share what you have written down.

    _____

    _____

    _____

3. What is one thing that someone in the family has done lately to hurt your feelings? Share what you have written down.

    _____

    _____

    _____

4. How do you think forgiveness could help your family situation? Share your ideas.

    _____

    _____

    _____

What forgiveness *is* and why it is a key to healing!

- Forgiveness *is* being able to release resentment because of what someone has done to hurt us.

- Forgiveness *is* a way to keep bitterness from building a firm foundation in our lives.

- Forgiveness *is* a way to be cleansed from anger, resentment or betrayal.

- Forgiveness *helps* to break the cycle of evil influences leading to wrong choices.

- Forgiveness *leads* to opportunities for positive change.

- Forgiveness *keeps* everyone spiritually healthy because of the grace of God.

- Forgiveness does not hold grudges but *leads* the way to setting good boundaries so repeat behaviors are eliminated.

- Forgiveness *is* a two-way action that benefits both the forgiver and the forgiven.

What forgiveness *is not* and why it *is* key to understanding!

- Forgiveness *is not* forgetting, but it can lead to greater awareness for future avoidance of offending.

- Forgiveness *is not* reconciliation. Reconciliation could be a long-range goal but by offering forgiveness, you get rid of the anger inside of you.

- Forgiveness *is not* agreeing with those who hurt you. It could look like you are condoning their offense, but although the offender can keep on offending, you no longer will tolerate hurtful behavior.

- Forgiveness *is not* a free ticket for others to keep on hurting you. Keeping a open dialogue to make offenders aware of their hurtful ways leads to greater opportunity for the offender to change for the better.

- Forgiveness *is not* a pardon. There may be consequences because of an offense but both parties can learn from the action of forgiving.

- Forgiveness *is not* a feeling. It is a conscious choice to forgive even when a person doesn't feel like it, but it could lead to less anxiety and greater joy.

What to ask?

4

 The Johnson family learned a lot from their sit-down family talk. What prevents you and your family from doing the same thing?

_____

_____

_____

_____

_____

 Has anyone in your family asked forgiveness for something they did that offended or hurt others in the family? What happened as a result?

_____

_____

_____

_____

 What is your understanding of the forgiveness process and of the benefits of forgiveness?

_____

_____

_____

_____

What to take away?

Note: LTC Johnson may be mad at God for the extra difficult deployment he just came home from. He saw much too much that seemed to be driving him further away from a son who needed him. Michael was feeling misunderstood and was deeply hurt that his father was not interested in his accomplishments. Both of them would benefit from clearing the air and acknowledging their need to trust each other. Working through a list of the points of pain and asking for and accepting forgiveness is a good start. The act of forgiving will be a great way to work through the pain each has in their hearts.

- The first step is to make a list of as many points of pain you can recall that hurt you deeply.

- Pray through each item something like this:

"Lord, I do not want to carry bitterness in my heart for the way _____ _____ has hurt me when he _____. Help me have a forgiving attitude and not harbor bitterness any longer. Thank You for cleansing my heart and guiding me today and in the future. I desire to be more obedient and allow You to help me grow in my faith. Amen."

- Know that when you calmly and peacefully tell someone how they hurt you, you have established an atmosphere that makes resolution possible.

- Know that when you have a forgiving heart, it benefits you and the one who has hurt you.

- Know that God desires you have a heart of love instead of anger.

Here's what forgiveness does:

1. It's the first step to healing.
2. It benefits everyone.
3. It releases unhealthy anger.
4. It frees the forgiver.
5. It helps the forgiven one make things right.
6. It can be a learned behavior.
7. It leads to asking forgiveness, if needed.

Here's how to forgive:

1. To ask for forgiveness, it is important to say the right words such as, "I am sorry. I was wrong. Will you forgive me for getting angry with you this morning?" (or for whatever the specific offense was).
2. To forgive someone, you could say the following, "I forgive you of your anger." (It is important to forgive even if you don't feel like it.)
3. What to say if you both need to ask forgiveness: "I forgive you. I am sorry. I was wrong for saying those bad words toward you too. Will you forgive me?" (Very good in giving the relationship a fresh start)
4. Always work on relationships so that bitterness does not have a hold on you and others.

What does God say?

Ephesians 4:32 – "Be kind to one another, tenderhearted, **forgiving** *one another, as God in Christ forgave you."*

Do you think this is possible to do? _____
Why or why not?

_____

_____

_____

What to pray?

"Lord, I choose to forgive those who hurt me and those with whom I am angry. Help me to forgive the hurtful words and actions that seem to be against me. Help me to be a better person who more easily forgives than holds grudges. Help me to be patient and kind instead of jumping to conclusions too fast. Thank You for forgiving me so I can have the strength to forgive. Amen."

What's next?

- Get all the facts first when someone is doing hurtful things against you. Michael's father may have been suffering from undiagnosed PTSD from multiple deployments resulting in a short fuse.

- Be willing to talk about what is happening instead of isolating or running away from situations. Michael could have gone to his mother to discuss how he was feeling. Michael's mother could have tried to seek professional help to determine what was happening to her husband. LTC Johnson could have confided in his family what he was feeling and thinking.

- In order for everyone in the Johnson family to continue on a positive path, a regular family talk time would give everyone opportunity to speak and to listen to each other.

Chapter 5

Meet the Jones family. Matt, the oldest of the four children, is a senior and graduates high school in a couple months. His two younger sisters, Sara and Carolyn, are the best 14- and 15-year-old soccer players in the area. Then there's Greg, who just turned 13. He loves to ride BMX bikes and races every weekend at the local race track. Mrs. Jones is a manager at the MCX on base. She has had a lot of retail experience and usually is able to find a job on base when they transfer to a new assignment.

Master Sergeant Jones returned not long ago from his latest deployment. He's always said how much he loves being in the military. He's worked in a variety of aviation jobs ever since reporting for service 18 years ago. For the most part everyone in the family has embraced the military lifestyle. They're proud of what their father has done for their country. That's why it was such a shock to the kids when they overheard their parents arguing behind the closed bedroom door. These arguments were becoming more and more frequent and their mom was becoming deeply depressed. She tried to hide her emotions but everyone saw that things were just not right.

It all came to a crisis the day MSGT Jones picked up the girls from soccer practice and decided to run a quick errand that took them into rush hour traffic on the freeway. It was stop-and-go driving, and he was cussing and yelling at the people who seemed to be doing their worst driving right in front of him. When he spotted a break in the flow of cars in the right lane, he began to make his move. But a little convertible sports car beat him to the punch, zooming in ahead of him. From the back seat, the girls were getting scared because their father was becoming more and more irate at the sports car's driver. He pulled up right next to it, lowered the passenger window and began to loudly cuss out the driver. The girls hadn't ever heard such language coming from their father. Sara told her dad to stop but he didn't listen.

>>>>>>>>>>>>>>>>>>>>>>>>>

When the sports car turned on a signal to take the next exit, MSGT Jones followed it off the freeway, hanging on to its bumper. The sports car turned into a gas station, the driver quickly parked and ran inside, talking on his cell phone. The girl's father drove on past the station but they were shaking. They were terrified of their father and his violent actions toward the other driver. As soon as the three arrived home, the girls ran into their room and locked the door. They took out a cell phone and called their mom at work to tell her what happened.

Mrs. Jones decided the family needed to feel safe at all times so she called the unit chaplain to confide in him what was happening. He listened intently and asked permission to contact the Family Advocacy for them. Mrs. Jones agreed because life was getting worse, not better. Her husband had come home from the latest deployment with a anger trigger level the family hadn't ever before experienced. The constant arguments and anger issues were not going away. Something had to be done.

5

What to learn?

Note: It is important that a thorough assessment is done for MSGT Jones to determine what is causing his increasingly angry outbursts and arguments. Once a counselor or therapist gets to the root cause and it is determined to be a result of Combat Trauma, treatment can begin. Bringing spiritual answers to the situation can lead to real healing.

What does God think about abuse or domestic violence?

1. God hates oppression, cruelty, abuse, and violence.
    Ezekiel 45:9

    _____

    _____

    _____

2. You are not your father's possession. If you are a Christian, you were bought by God with the blood of Jesus Christ and belong to Him.
    1 Corinthians 6:19,20

    _____

    _____

    _____

3. It is your father's responsibility to take care of you and provide for your needs, not neglect you and make your life more difficult.
1 Timothy 5:8

_____

_____

_____

4. If your father treats you disrespectfully, he will experience resistance from God.
Isaiah 58:4

_____

_____

_____

5. The violence people practice will eventually backfire.
Psalm 7:16

_____

_____

_____

6. God forbids verbal abuse and name-calling.
Ephesians 4:29

_____

_____

_____

7. God expects a father to respect and honor his children.
Ephesians 6:4

_____

_____

_____

_____

What to ask?

5

 Q.1 A loved one, just back from deployment, is displaying some unusual behaviors which are causing others in the family to be afraid for their safety. At what point should any family member report these actions?

_____

_____

Who should be notified? _____

_____

 Q.2 Has your family ever experienced some kind of abuse caused by a loved one became increasingly violent after returning from combat?_____
What did you do?

_____

_____

_____

_____

 Q.3 Did the experience with abuse or violence send you to find help from God or drive you away from seeking God's help? _____ What happened?

_____

_____

_____

_____

What to take away?

What are some of the different forms of abuse?

- **Emotional Abuse.** An intentional or unintentional **attack** on another person's character, worth or abilities to gain a position of superiority, power and control through s*hame, insult, ridicule, intimidation, embarrassment, or demeaning.*

- **Verbal Abuse.** Intentionally or unintentionally using **words** to gain a position of superiority, power and control over another person through: *withholding, countering, discounting, malicious jokes, blocking/diverting, judging/criticizing, trivializing, undermining, threatening, name-calling, forgetting, ordering/ demanding.*

- **Physical Abuse.** Any act, physical force or **violence** that is done to coerce or gain a position of superiority, power and control which results in bodily injury, pain or impairment through: *shoving, hitting, kicking, slapping, grabbing, shaking, manhandling, cutting, biting, burning, blocking, striking with an object, exposure to heat, cold or electrical shock, exposure to a toxic substance or disease, negligence, or withholding food or medicines.*

- **Sexual Abuse. Forcing** someone to engage in sexual acts or touching when he or she does not want to.

What are some of the danger signs of abuse?

> Note: Check the danger signs you have noticed in your family exhibited by someone who may be suffering from PTSD/TBI. If five or more have been checked discuss the situation with a pastor, chaplain or counselor for the next steps you should take.

- ☐ Born and raised in a violent family
- ☐ Use of violence to solve problems
- ☐ Abuse of alcohol and drugs
- ☐ Poor opinion of self, which brings about a 'tough guy' image
- ☐ Often acts jealously
- ☐ Acts authoritarian
- ☐ Emotionally attacks people with a critical spirit

What are some of the danger signs of abuse?

☐ Appears to have a "Jekyll and Hyde" personality

☐ Controls who family members can talk to, hang out with, be friends with

☐ Intimidates through a look, angry outburst, gesture or display of weapons

☐ Uses threats to coerce someone to do something

☐ Minimizes his bad behavior by mocking and blaming everyone but himself

☐ Is financially irresponsible and wants to control all the money

☐ Always has a weapon nearby

☐ Has a previous history of violence

☐ Cannot accept rejection and is inflexible

☐ Believes others are out to get him

☐ Usually moody and sullen

☐ Has vivid flashbacks from combat experiences

☐ Becomes destructive when angry

What does God say?

*Psalm 40:2 – "He drew me up from the pit of destruction, out of the miry bog, and set my feet upon a rock, making my steps **secure**."*

Do you believe God can change a violent person? _____
Why or why not?

_____

_____

_____

_____

What to pray?

"Lord, I call upon You to help me and my family so we will be kept safe from any harm. Help my father learn how to control his anger and be healed from his afflictions. Make him the kind of person you want him to be: loving, kind, and forgiving. Help each one of us reach out to You for the help we need to be a family that turns to You for guidance and encouragement. Amen."

What's next?

- Design a family plan either to get help or escape continual abuse.

- Have a central place for family members to go to if necessary.

- Call important friends who are aware of the situation to ask them to pray, pick up the children, contact authorities, or contact a chaplain, lawyer etc.

- Keep a diary of any and every type of abuse inflicted on anyone in the family.

- Be willing to reach out for help so every family member can feel secure and feel loved in spite of the situation in the home. Contact your Family Readiness Officer, Family Advocacy Program, Family Support Office, MilitaryOneSource.mil, or other websites such as MilitaryReadyFamily.org for extra resources.

Chapter 6

"Where can I go for help?"

Healing

Meet the Lee family. The four teenagers in the family were invited to a concert by the youth group leader at the church they occasionally attend. Kevin, an outstanding musician, just turned 17. The twins, Jack and Sally, are 16 and both excel academically. The youngest of the Lee children is Anne, who will be celebrating her 14th birthday in two weeks. Her time has been taken up with planning a fun party with all of her friends.

But ever since the family heard about the injuries their father suffered in combat, most of the family's focus has been on getting him 100% healthy again. Six months has gone by since he had been flown to Germany and then to the U.S. for treatment. It had been an intense time for everyone as they coordinated hospital visits with their regular busy schedules. The nearby Wounded Warrior battalion had some great facilities where their father spent his days recovering and recuperating through daily physical therapy. The injuries to both his legs were severe and for a while they didn't know if he would walk again.

Going to the concert gave the Lee teenagers a break from the daily stresses of life. All of the teens in the youth group had been looking forward to the concert for weeks. Mark, the youth group leader, was ecstatic to see the Lees show up for the bus ride especially knowing what they'd been going through with their father's recovery. He knew the music and message of the Gospel would touch their hearts and hopefully bring some healing. He wasn't quite sure if any of the Lee kids had ever established a relationship with God since they came only sporadically to the weekly youth group meetings at the church.

The week after the inspiring concert, Kevin made an appointment with Mark to ask some questions he'd been having. He'd been reading the book of John in his Bible to learn more about why Jesus had died on the cross. The message proclaimed at the concert was similar to what he was reading but it still didn't make sense to him. While digging through his backpack one day, he'd pulled out a little booklet he picked up at church explaining how to become a Christian. He brought it with him to the appointment hoping to get answers to all his questions.

>>>>>>>>>>>>>>>>>>>>>>>>>

What to learn?

6

> Note: Here is a summary of the discussion Kevin had with Mark, the youth leader from church.

Kevin: "Why is it so important for me to ask Jesus into my heart?"

Mark: "It shows God you are serious about knowing how much He loves you and your family. In John 3:16 it says, *'For God so loved the world, that He gave His only Son, that whoever believes in Him should not perish but have eternal life.'* He's had a plan all along to establish a personal and loving relationship, through Jesus, with all who live on this earth."

Kevin: "What's keeping me from having a relationship with God?"

Mark: "Well, all people sin which means they've turned their back on God and those they sin against. Isaiah 59:2 says, *'But your iniquities have made a separation between you and your God, and your sins have hidden His face from you so that He does not hear.'* Sin acts like a barrier between you and God if you don't take care of it."

Kevin: "How do I do that?"

Mark: "That's where Jesus comes into the picture. God sent Him to earth to pay for all the sins anyone has ever committed. Romans 5:8 states, *'but God shows His love for us in that while we were still sinners, Christ died for us.'* God's plan was for Jesus to die on the cross to pay the penalty for all of our sins. Another verse that is important to know is found in John 14:6, *'Jesus said to him, "I am the way, and the truth and the life. No one comes to the Father except through Me."'* Even though this may be hard to understand, it is really the first step in leading a life that is great to live."

Kevin: "What happens if I ask Jesus into my heart?"

Mark: "The first thing that happens is that your sins are forgiven - past, present and future. Jesus' death paid for all of the sins of mankind. The second thing is that it shows you are choosing to give your life over to the will of God and His plan for your life. Ephesians 2:8,9 reads, *'For by grace you have been saved through faith. And this is not your own doing; it is the gift of God, not a result of works, so that no one may boast.'* Does that make sense?"

Kevin: "Kinda. So what do I say to begin this relationship with Jesus and God?"

Mark: "It doesn't really matter exactly what you say but it might sound like this:

'Lord Jesus, I want to know You personally. Thank You for dying on the cross for me and giving me eternal life. Thank You for forgiving all of my sins. I believe You are the way, the truth and the life. Make me the kind of person who trusts in Your work in my life forever. Amen.'

"Does this prayer express the desire of your heart?"

Kevin: "Yes, it all makes sense to me now. Should I pray it now?"

Mark: "How about I say it line by line and you can repeat it after me?"

Kevin: "Yes, that's cool! I'll do it!"

Mark: "Let's pray!"

What to ask?

Note: Kevin was ready to understand why it was important to ask Jesus into his heart even though he was not sure what the result would be. That is called faith. Be honest and truthful when answering the following questions.

Q.1 Have you ever begun a personal relationship with Jesus by asking Him to come into your life with a prayer similar to the one Kevin prayed? _____ Tell your story.

_____

_____

_____

_____

_____

Q.2 If you have not prayed a prayer like that before, what has kept you from doing that?

_____

_____

_____

_____

 Q.3 What questions do you need answered before you commit to asking Jesus into your heart?

_____

_____

_____

_____

6

What to take away?

How will I know Jesus is in my life?

- In Revelation 3:20 Jesus says, *"Behold, I stand at the door and knock. If anyone hears My voice and opens the door, I will come in to him and eat with him, and he with Me."*

- Jesus said He would come in to your life and because He is trustworthy, you can count on it being done.

- The authority of God found throughout the Bible is enough to prove to you that He keeps His promises.

How will I know I have eternal life?

- In 1 John 5:11-13 it reads, *"And this is the testimony, that God gave us eternal life, and this life is in His Son. Whoever has the Son has life; whoever does not have the Son of God does not have life. I write these things to you who believe in the name of the Son of God that you may <u>know</u> that you have eternal life."*

- Based on the promise of God, when you pray to invite Jesus into your life, you also immediately receive eternal life.

- Now that Jesus is in your life, He will be there forever and never leave you.

How should this decision make me feel?

- You should live by faith in the trustworthiness of God Himself and His Word, not on your feelings.

- You should live your life on the authority and promises found in God's Word.

- Your faith in God should be reflected by obedience to God's Word as found in John 14:21, where Jesus is speaking, *"Whoever has My commandments and keeps them, he it is who loves Me. And he who loves Me will be loved by My Father; and I will love him and manifest Myself to him."*

How will my life change because Christ is in it?

- You'll know Christ will be with you forever.

- You'll know your sins - past, present and future - are forgiven.

- You've become a child of God.

- You've received eternal life.

- You can go to God in prayer anywhere and anytime.

- You can witness for Christ with your life and your words.

- You can trust God for every detail of your life.

- You have been empowered by the gift of the Holy Spirit (see Chapter 7).

- You can find fellowship with others who believe in Jesus.

What does God say?

Psalm 41:4 – "As for me, I said, 'O Lord, be gracious to me; **heal** *me, for I have sinned against you.' "*

Do you believe God can heal?_____ Why or why not?

_____

_____

_____

_____

What to pray?

"Lord, our family's life and schedule have been turned upside down in the last few months. I come before You to thank You for taking me into the family of God and making me a child of Yours. Help everyone in my family see the need for You in their lives too. I pray You will heal our hearts and my dad's body from the effects of war. Help us surrender our lives to Your plans for us. Amen."

6

What's next?

Note: Kevin wants to start his walk as a Christian the right way. A good way to do that is to be involved in a group Bible study. The chart below shows the beginning steps. Look up the verses under the *Why?* column and list the answer of *How?* you would act upon the words of the verses.

WHAT?	WHY?	HOW?
Study God's Word	John 8:31.32	
Pray about everything	Philippians 4:6	
Share my story	John 9:18-27	
Serve others	Galatians 5:13	
Keep my way pure	Psalm 119:9,11	

Chapter 7

"What should I do first?"

Confessing

Meet the White family. After Mr. White retired from the military ten years earlier, he started his own construction company bidding on projects all over the world. During his military career, he and his family had lived in countries on several continents. They loved the international aspect of his work, especially connecting with other cultures. Mr. White's education and experience in structural engineering made him a perfect fit for the projects he has been a part of overseas. To 18-year-old Jessica, his only child, accepting her father's periodic absences for most of her growing up years seemed normal. But something had changed in the last year. Her father's personality had changed after returning from a difficult project based in one of the war-torn countries.

There seemed to be an unexplained tension in the air usually characterized by silent pauses in conversations when both parents were in the same room. Jessica knew something was wrong, and she finally decided to approach her mom about it. She wanted to find out what was causing the deafening silence and taking her mom to lunch at their favorite restaurant was a perfect chance to spend quality time together, just to talk. When they sat down, Jessica could hardly wait until the waitress finally took the order and walked away. "Mom, what is going on between you and Dad? I've noticed a big difference in Dad since he came home from overseas."

Jessica's mom didn't say a word before tears started streaming down her cheeks. She grabbed some tissue out of her purse and blew her nose. She said she had been trying to figure out what to do for several weeks. She hadn't wanted to burden her daughter with it, as it was Jessica's first year in college and she already had so many adjustments to make. She told Jessica that her dad wasn't the same since he returned from that last project and he hasn't said what happened over there to make him so sad and withdrawn. His change in behavior was a mystery to her, and she did not know whom to turn to for help.

Jessica realized this would be a good opportunity to let her mom hear about some of the amazing discoveries she has made while studying the Bible. She'd been wanting to tell her parents about all she has been learning through the Christian group she meets with on campus every week. Her parents attended the neighborhood church sporadically. Jessica had learned about the Christian life in the church's youth group. Now in college, her small group meets every week to study the Bible together. They have fun and participate in weekly inspirational meetings, and she's been learning how to tell others about what is happening in her life because she knows Jesus Christ.

She had brought a little booklet called *Have You Made the Wonderful Discovery of the Spirit-Filled Life?* to the lunch with her mom, in case she would be open to looking at it. Somehow, Jessica felt this is just the kind of information that would help her mom and dad during this rough time in their marriage.

What to learn?

Note: Jessica knew her mother believed in Jesus and had prayed to invite Him into her life several years earlier, but she was not sure about her father. She wanted both her mom and dad to hear how to truly follow Christ. She opened the little booklet she had been studying lately and asked if she could share it with her mom. Jessica knew the information could change the family dynamics forever. Follow along with Jessica as she tells her mom about the simple yet powerful truth found in the pages.

Jessica: "Mom, have you ever heard about 'spiritual breathing'?"

Mom: "Not sure what you mean. I have never heard or read about it before. What does this have to do with Dad and his attitude?"

Jessica: "What I'm going to share with you is one of the most important concepts to understand in the Christian life. In my small group at college, we have been studying about this quite a bit lately. It has given me a whole new perspective about how to live my life, no matter what comes my way."

Mom: "Tell me about what you are learning."

Jessica: "First, let's look at the three kinds of people the Bible describes. First, 1 Corinthians 2:14 talks about the 'Natural Person.' This is one who has not yet received Christ. Look at this circle. Self is on the throne and Christ is outside the life. The person is directing their own interests (the dots), which results in confusion, frustration and despair, because they are in discord with God's plan.

"Mom, you told me a few years ago you had asked Jesus into your heart at the woman's retreat you went to, right?"

Mom: "Yes, but that was so long ago, and lately, I haven't felt very close to God."

Jessica: "Look at this next circle, Mom. It shows what a life that is Christ-directed looks like. 1 Corinthians 1:15,16 calls this the 'Spiritual Person.' Christ is on the throne and Self is yielding to Him. The person's interests are directed by Christ and are in harmony with God's plan.

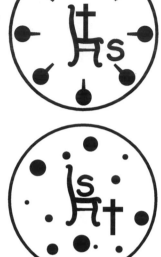

Mom: "Even though I invited Christ into my life, I guess I have not been pursuing what it truly means to understand the Christian life. With my job and your dad's absences, I didn't really like going to church by myself so I didn't get involved."

Jessica: "Let me tell you about the third kind of person, "People of the Flesh,' also called a 'Worldly Christian.' This person, described in 1 Corinthians 3:1-3, tends to live a defeated life because she is trying to live the Christian life in her own strength. You can see by the dots in this circle, that things are not going right. Christ is still in the life but Self is not yielding control to Him.

"Mom, when a person is yielding her life to Christ and allowing the Holy Spirit's power to work, her life shows some of the following:

- Love
- Joy
- Peace
- Patience
- Empowered by the Holy Spirit
- Introduces others to Christ

- Kindness
- Faithfulness
- Goodness
- Christ-centered

- Effective prayer life
- Understands God's Word
- Trusts God
- Obeys God

"I've learned that most Christians are not experiencing what is called the abundant life because they haven't learned to turn to God for everything. From the moment we become believers in Christ, we have the Holy Spirit living in us. Not all Christians know how to be directed and empowered by the Holy Spirit all the time. That's where 'spiritual breathing' comes in."

Mom: "I was wondering when you were going to tell me about what that meant."

Jessica: "I learned that spiritual breathing involves letting out the old air or sin and taking in the pure air which is Christ's forgiveness, but it takes a conscious effort to practice this. For instance, remember today when we were driving here and I got angry with the man who cut me off on the freeway and I said a few choice words about him? That was not a good reflection of Christ living in me. Remember me saying, 'Lord, I have a bad attitude. Please, forgive me and help me not react like that again.' I asked for forgiveness and asked the Lord to change my attitude. I admitted my sin, asked for God's forgiveness and His help in not reacting with anger. The anger was only hurting me and keeping me from living victoriously."

Mom: "What does this have to do with the situation with Dad?"

Jessica: "When we try to solve our own problems and not turn to God for help, it keeps us from allowing the Spirit of God to work in and through us."

Mom: "I see. You are saying I am upset about what is happening with Dad and I'm not turning to God for help. I need to be more trusting of Him to give me answers instead of trying to figure everything out myself. Do I understand what you are saying?"

Jessica: "Yes! Spiritual Breathing for you right now would be asking God to forgive you for not trusting Him with this situation. Then you would thank Him for forgiving you for your unbelief. The power of the Holy Spirit will immediately begin to work, but you must believe He will do that. Ephesians 5:18 says, *'and do not get drunk with wine, for that is debauchery, but be filled with the Spirit.'* My small group leader taught me that, the way this is written, it is a command from God."

Mom: "It seems I have a lot to learn about the way God wants to work in my life."

Jessica: "Another important verse is found in 1 John 5:14,15. God has given us many promises especially when it comes to prayer. *'And this is the confidence that we have toward Him, that if we ask anything according to His will He hears us. And if we know that He hears us in whatever we ask, we know that we have the requests that we have asked of Him.'*

Mom: "What exactly do I say to God? I don't quite get what I should say."

Jessica: "Well, the first thing you'll want to do is pray and ask to be filled with the Holy Spirit. When I learned about this concept in the Christian life, I prayed a prayer like this one:

'Dear Father God, I need Your help, I agree with You that I am not trusting You and I have not asked You to direct all the activities in my life. You have forgiven me as a result of Christ's death on the cross. I want to invite Christ to be the one that is on the throne of my life. Fill me with the Holy Spirit as You commanded me to be filled, and as You promised in Your Word that You would do if I asked in faith. I want to trust You and believe You will give me hope in our family situation. Thank You for directing my life and for filling me with the Holy Spirit. Amen.'

7

Mom: "So, first I acknowledge that I need to turn to God for everything in prayer. He will hear my prayers and the Holy Spirit will guide me to answers from the Lord because of what Jesus Christ did on the cross when He died. Wow, it is amazing to think about all the possibilities of seeing how God can work in our lives."

Jessica: "Yes, it is very exciting and I believe our whole family will benefit from the power of the Holy Spirit working in each one of us. Do you want to pray this prayer right now, Mom?"

Mom: "Oh, yes!"

What to ask?

Note: Answer the following questions truthfully but remember to be respectful of each other and your family members. Be a good listener. Do not share or repeat anything you hear outside the group. Confidentiality helps make the group a safe place to share from your heart. Everyone should be made to feel accepted no matter what. Everyone should feel open to sharing as this gives hope to those who speak. Sharing God's love and His Word brings encouragement and transformed lives.

 Have you ever heard of what it means to live a Spirit-filled life? If so, what did it mean to you?

_____

_____

_____

 Do you find it difficult to think Christ on the throne of your life will give you a more abundant life? Why or why not?

_____

_____

_____

 What activities would be easy to give to Christ and what activities would be too hard to give over to Him?

_____

_____

_____

What to take away?

Note: The person who says they are a Christian but continues to practice sin should realize it is a dangerous position to be in. True Christians would not want to continue down the path of sin: *"No one who abides in Him keeps on sinning; no one who keeps on sinning has either seen Him or known Him. Little children, let no one deceive you. Whoever practices righteousness is righteous, as He is righteous. Whoever makes a practice of sinning is of the devil, for the devil has been sinning from the beginning. The reason the Son of God appeared was to destroy the works of the devil. No one born of God makes a practice of sinning, for God's seed abides in Him, and he cannot keep on sinning because he has been born of God.* (1 John 3:6-9)"

Some or all of the following traits may characterize the **Worldly Christian** who does not fully trust God. In the quietness of your heart, if there are traits you find in your life, now is the time to ask forgiveness, turn your back on that trait and ask God to fill you with the goodness of the Holy Spirit and put Christ on the throne of your life.

Legalistic attitude	Aimlessness
Impure thoughts	Fear
Jealousy	Ignorance of spiritual heritage
Guilt	Unbelief
Worry	Disobedience
Discouragement	Loss of love for God and others
Critical spirit	Poor prayer life
Frustration	No desire for Bible study

What does God say?

*1 John 1:9,10 – "If we **confess** our sins, He is faithful and just to forgive us our sins and to cleanse us from all unrighteousness. If we say we have not sinned, we make Him a liar, and His Word is not in us."*

Are you willing to turn to God for help with your whole life?_____
Make it a priority to deepen your relationship with God by praying and studying His Word. What is keeping you from making the best decision of your life?

_____

_____

What to pray?

"Lord, keep me from being deceived any longer. Thank you for all of the plans You have put in place so I can live a great life filled with righteousness. Make me turn to You immediately whenever I encounter the bumps and turns of life. Help me focus on what is the truth in the world I live in and not on the lies of the deceiver. Help me to not let my feelings get in the way so my faith in You is strong. I love You! Amen."

What's next?

Note: Being your own person is important. The choices you make every day will determine whether you have a day filled with stress or peace. Here are some ideas to keep you on the right track:

- Practice having a "quiet time" (spending time alone in God's Word or inspirational readings).
- Prayer keeps the communication open between you and God.
- Bible Study opens your mind and heart to becoming a mature Christian.
- Find a prayer partner you can confide in and pray with.
- Find ways to reach out to others using your strengths and passions in life.
- Schedule fun and wholesome activities.
- Prioritize everything and learn how to say "No" to busyness.
- Hang out with people you trust; who encourage you.

Chapter 8

"Does anyone care?"

Seeking

Meet the Perez family. Teenagers Tomas, 17 years old, Gabriel, 16 years old and Rachel, 14 years old are seasoned travelers. They have all experienced living overseas when their father was stationed abroad. The first overseas assignment their father had was in Germany many years ago. Tomas, Gabriel and Rachel loved living in Germany and all learned to speak German. Going to the international school helped them make friends from all over the world.

The second assignment overseas was on a base out of Spain. Because their father was an expert in guidance missiles, and had just completed a master's degree in financial management, his expertise was a valuable asset to the team in Spain. Again, the teenagers adapted very well to the move and loved the schools they attended. Every year they looked forward to traveling all around Europe during their holidays. The family rule was that they had to get at least a B average on their report cards to be able to go on the trips. Their mom and dad wanted them to experience as many cultures as possible to help them receive a proper world view from the countries they visited. The teenagers never missed a trip because they all did very well in their studies.

Now that they are living in the States again, each member of the Perez family has heard stories of families that are dealing with issues concerning Combat Trauma. Just last night at the dinner table, their mom told about a lady she met at the hair salon where she works, who knows there is something wrong with her husband. He just came back from being deployed for eight months but is not the same man who left to go on the assignment. The lady is beside herself with trying to figure out what to do or who to ask for help.

Additionally, the kids' high school recently had a special speaker panel for an assembly. The topic of the panel discussion was how to understand the issues of Post-Traumatic Stress Disorder (PTSD). There were so many students who had questions for the speakers afterwards, they promised to come back for just a

question-and-answer assembly. Tomas was especially interested in learning more about the subject. He decided to write a report for his next English assignment on how PTSD affects the whole family.

The church the Perez family attends has a vital ministry to the military, both to active duty as well as veterans of military service from all eras. Tomas decided to make an appointment with the director of the church's Military Ministry to do some background research for his report. What he discovered gave him a change of desire and focus for his upcoming college education. He decided to become a counselor specializing in Combat Trauma and how it affects the whole family. As he learned about what so many have been experiencing, who were wounded in body and spirit through multiple deployments, he came up with a plan to get more teenagers involved in reaching out to hurting families. He knew his brother and sister would be the first ones to join this cause and couldn't wait till dinner time to share all the ideas with his family.

What to learn?

8

Note: The first thing Tomas did was go to his principal at school to explain his idea about starting a support group for teens whose parents are suffering from some kind of Combat Trauma. In his research, he learned the whole family is affected in different ways and there should be help out there for each member. He wanted to figure out what was needed to start a support group for teenagers from military families. After much research, he wrote out a proposal to present to the principal during his appointment. He thought that if the principal said no, he could start a support group through the Youth Group program at his local church.

The Triple Win Club Proposal

Mission Statement: *The Triple Win Club* wishes to become a safe haven for teens of all ages in military families where they can express feelings, be accepted and nurtured through the family difficulties brought on by Combat Trauma issues.

Vision: *The Triple Win Club* is available to provide teens information leading to potential understanding, support from a caring community of peers and guidance in offering resources for the whole family.

73

Community Service: *The Triple Win Club* wishes to become an option for 100 hours of supervised volunteering in order to qualify for college applications.

On-site Supervisor: *The Triple Win Club* wishes to have approval from school leadership appointing a supervising teacher or administrator to sign volunteer verification forms at the end of school year.

Student and Parent Surveys: *The Triple Win Club* would like to conduct surveys for the military families and students represented in our school to gain information on best topics and ways to present services.

Student Committee Formation: *The Triple Win Club* would like to appoint a committee of military-minded students who will form the leadership of the club.

Rules, Regulations and Policies: *The Triple Win Club* leadership committee will be responsible for establishing, implementing and carrying out the rules, regulations and policies with the approval of the principal and on-site supervisor.

Facts about PTSD:

- 2.2% of the U.S. Population are affected by PTSD (317 million).
- 10% of women and 5% of men will develop PTSD in their lifetime.
- 55-70% of the population will experience a traumatic event in their lifetime.
- 7-8% of the population will experience PTSD at some point in their lifetime.
- 11-20% of all veterans of Iraq and Afghanistan wars suffer from PTSD. Two-thirds of Iraq and Afghanistan veterans suffering from PTSD may not be receiving treatment.
- 10% of all Gulf War veterans suffer from PTSD.
- 30% of all Vietnam veterans suffer from PTSD.
- 24% of Korean War soldiers who saw direct combat were discharged for psychiatric reasons.
- 37% of WWII soldiers who saw direct combat were discharged for psychiatric reasons.

*Above statistics taken from www.militarymentalhealth.org

Resources: *The Triple Win Club* will use all resources available based on the Equal Access Act. Included in the resources will be special speakers, books, study guides which may or may not contain religious information.

First Steps:

- Form leadership committee of military-minded students.
- Recruit at least one faculty member as a sponsor.
- Raise funds from the local community for promotion, materials and food.
- Recruit parents who can provide assistance in raising funds, services, and transportation when needed.
- Determine place, date and time to meet.
- Design a survey for students and parents to gather information.

What to ask?

 Q.1 Has your family or someone you know been affected by PTSD in some way? _____
How? _____

_____

_____

 Q.2 How much do you understand about PTSD? _____
Are you willing to learn more about it? _____

_____

_____

 Q.3 Have you considered joining a group of peers who are experiencing traumatic stress because of a loved one who has served in a war zone? _____
Why or why not? _____

_____

_____

What to take away?

What can be expected of a peer support group?

- To provide a safe place to share thoughts, feelings and needs
- To give support in dealing with problems related to PTSD
- To be good listeners so everyone is heard
- To learn how to be good friends to others but not try to fix them
- To keep confidential everything that is said
- To share only facts and not gossip about others
- To learn how to make best choices
- To learn healthy communication skills

What is expected of a peer support leader?

- As a leader serving on the committee, learn all you can about PTSD.
- Realize confidentiality is crucial for everyone to feel safe.
- Hang in there for the long haul especially when hurting students are reacting to their situation. Try to remain calm and reassuring.
- Be consistent in praying for the lives you touch.
- Be proactive in finding ways to be kind and compassionate.
- Have a good support team in place and take turns reaching out.
- Be ready to ask for necessary help when a crisis is too difficult.
- Be open to God's leading for you to be an encourager and speak the truth.

How does God help us in reaching out to those in need?

What the Bible says	Ideas for using it	Application for you
A friend loves at all times, and a brother is born for adversity **Proverbs 17:17**	Write down names of those you will stand by, no matter what.	
It is more blessed to give than to receive. **Acts 20:35b**	Think of opportunities to bless those in need of your friendship.	
Let every person be quick to hear, slow to speak, slow to anger. **James 1:19b**	Practice being a good listener, who does not interrupt others with a bigger story to tell.	
Iron sharpens iron, and one man sharpens another. **Proverbs 27:17**	Be intentional in assisting others to choose a healing process that is positive.	
But exhort one another every day, as long as it is called "today," that none of you may be hardened by the deceitfulness of sin. **Hebrews 3:13**	Think of ways to encourage for the long haul by being positive and supportive, especially by complimenting good behavior.	
The effective prayer of a righteous person has great power. **James 5:16b**	Start a prayer journal and be consistent in writing down and praying for those you help.	
Be kind to one another, tenderhearted, forgiving one another, as God In Christ forgave you. **Ephesians 4:32**	Trust that God will use you in the lives of those He brings your way. Be a good witness for Him.	

What does God say?

*Jeremiah 29:13 – "You will **seek** Me and find Me,
when you **seek** Me with all your heart."*

Are you seeking God as you look for ways to reach out to others in need?

_____

If not, what are some ways you can make changes to improve your relationship skills to make a lasting difference in the lives you touch?

_____

_____

_____

What to pray?

"Lord, help me be the kind of friend who brings honor to Your name and is a bridge to those who don't know You and Your power to heal. Give me ideas of how to reach out to those around me who are hurting because of Combat Trauma in their lives. I trust You to help me be a better listener and friend. Amen."

What's next?

Helpful information to pass along

- www.crumilitary.org Cru Military website full of resources
- www.aacc.net American Association of Christian Counselors
- www.focusonthefamily.com List of nationwide network of counselors
- www.al-anon.org Website for family members of alcoholics
- www.aa.org Alcoholics Anonymous
- www.hopeforthehomefront.com Website for hurting families

Chapter 9

"Is what I do important?"

Focus

Meet the Wells family. Sandra is an only child to her parents, William and Mary Wells. She was born in Japan while her father served in the military as an air traffic controller. Over the years, he has served in units mostly related to anything that has to do with airplanes and air travel. Sandra has heard her mother speak about her husband's job to friends, with an explanation something like this, "William has been trained to make quick decisions using his math skills while under extreme pressure to keep all of the aircraft and people on the ship or ground safe from danger."

Sandra has always had trouble talking to her dad since he has been absent from the family scene for so many milestones in her life. Her mom has always worked before and after she was born. Her abilities as an experienced Certified Public Accountant (CPA) have always helped her get good jobs wherever they have lived in the world. For much of Sandra's growing up years, she has gone to day care or was a part of an after-school program. Because she was very bright, she was able to get her homework done so quickly, and thus began to escape her lonely life by reading 2-3 books per week.

William Wells had a reserved personality and could be classified as a loner-type so it was no surprise that Sandra did not mind escaping her real life with the life of make-believe she found in the books she devoured. The family has lived all over the world but now find themselves at a base in the States. The latest move seems to have put Sandra into even more of a shell until just lately.

>>>>>>>>>>>>>>>>>>>>>>>>>>>

The Wells family had been at their latest assignment for a little over a year now. Sandra was a junior in high school and during the first week of school she walked home with a girl who lived right next door. Michelle and Sandra had two classes together, and they discovered they both had a love for reading books and writing. They became instant friends and spent almost every day either at one or the other's home. If Sandra was not at Michelle's, she was in her room with the door closed.

Ever since their daughter became friends with Michelle, Sandra's parents began to notice a change in how she seemed to perceive herself and the world around her.

One day recently, while Sandra had gone on an errand with her father, Michelle came knocking on the front door to return a book she had borrowed. After inviting her in to chat a bit, Sandra's mom asked Michelle a question about what made the difference in her life because she always seemed to be so happy. She told Michelle she has noticed some really great changes in her daughter since the two of them had become inseparable friends. What started out as one question turned into a deep conversation that surprised a mom who was not ready for the answers she heard to her inquiry.

9

What to learn?

Note: Michelle explained about a class at her church in which she was learning a lot about the difference between the lies of Satan and how God views her and her classmates. She told Mrs. Wells that the Biblical truths she was memorizing gave her ammunition to resist the temptation to believe the lies. She and the other teens have been practicing positive talk, positive thoughts, and positive behavior in order to change how they view each other. She admitted she had been practicing what she had learned with Sandra in the last few weeks. She hoped that was okay!! Now it is your turn to take the time to look up each verse and write the positive statement the truth in the Bible reveals.

Satan's Lie	Verses	God's Truth	Positive Statement about Me!
No one wants to know you.	Ephesians 1:4	Ex. God loves you and chose you.	Ex. I am known, loved and chosen by God before He made the world!
You should go sit on the sidelines.	Matthew 5:14		
You are unforgivable.	Romans 8:1		
You are absolutely worthless.	1 Peter 1:18,19		
Everyone else is better than you.	1 Peter 2:4,5		
You can't do anything right.	1 John 5:4,5		
You are so ugly and boring.	Romans 5:8		
You are alone and you should stay that way.	1 Corinthians 12:27		

82

What to ask?

Q.1 Have you or someone in your family been deceived by Satan's lies? _____
How has it affected this person's personality? _____

_____

_____

Q.2 How would you describe the feelings you experience as a result of being deceived
by Satan's lies? Choose any words that describe your state of mind:

☐ frustrated   ☐ helpless   ☐ worthless

☐ confused   ☐ depressed   ☐ unimportant

☐ fearful   ☐ unmotivated   ☐ _____

☐ lack of power   ☐ ineffective   ☐ _____

Q.3 What needs to change in your life so you will not linger along Satan's path of
destruction and deception?

_____

_____

_____

_____

9

What to take away?

This is Who I Am

Regarded

I am a friend of the Almighty God of heaven and earth (John 15:15).

Jesus is not ashamed to call me His brother or sister (Hebrews 2:11).

I am chosen by God, holy and without fault in His eyes (Ephesians 1:4).

I am an heir to the riches of the Creator of the universe (Galatians 4:7).

Important

I have been rightly called a child of God (John 1:12).

God has made me His salt and light in the world (Matthew 5:13,14).

I am an eternal being and will never perish (John 3:16).

Forgiven

I am no longer condemned (Romans 8:1).

I have been justified before the righteous Judge (Romans 5:1a).

I am at peace with God (Romans 5:1b).

God no longer remembers my sins (Hebrews 10:17).

Valued

God loves me with an everlasting love (Jeremiah 31:3).

I am God's temple, bought at a great price (1 Corinthians 6:19,20).

God knows, chose, called, justified and glorified me (Romans 8:29,30).

Accepted

I am accepted in Christ (Romans 15:7).

I am chosen, costly, a living stone in God's building (1 Peter 2:4,5).

I have bold, unrestricted access to God's throne of grace (Hebrews 4:16).

Powerful

God has given me the spirit of power, love and a sound mind (2 Timothy 1:7).

God's Spirit in me is greater than any unholy spirits in the world (1 John 4:4).

I am born of God and believe in Jesus. I'm a world-overcomer (1 John 5:4,5).

Lovable

I am loved by God and nothing will keep us apart (Romans 8:38,39).

I am loved supremely – enough for God to die for me (John 15:13).

I am loved unconditionally, even when I sin (Romans 5:8).

Connected

I am intimately attached to Christ and bearing fruit (John 15:5).

I am a member of God's eternal family (Galatians 3:26).

Christ is as close to me as my heart and lungs (Galatians 2:20).

I am part of Christ's body with millions of brothers and sisters (1 Corinthians 12:27).

I am an eternal member of God's Kingdom and household (Ephesians 2:19).

9

What does God say?

Ephesians 4:25 – "Therefore, having put away falsehood,
let each one of you speak the **truth** with his neighbor,
for we are members one of another."

Are you honest with your family and friends in how you speak to them and treat them? ___

How can you practice speaking the truth in a positive way to your friends and family? List several ideas on the lines below:

_____

_____

_____

_____

_____

What to pray?

"Lord, thank You for the way You have made me. Help me be the kind of person who seeks to know You better so I can be a positive influence on those I know. Thank You for the many blessings and promises I have because Jesus Christ died on the cross for me. Thank You for the gift of the Holy Spirit at work in my life to help me when Satan has deceived me with lies. Thank You for Your love. Amen."

What's next?

Bad Practices	Good Practices
Ignore people we don't understand.	Reach out to family or friends.
Believe lies that no one cares.	Believe God loves and cares for me.
Complain about everything.	Always keep a positive attitude.
Focus only on negative circumstances.	Focus on the truths found in the Bible.
Keep a hardened heart.	Have a forgiving heart.
Be too busy to study the Bible.	Study the Bible with a group of peers.
Stay mad when I am angry.	Look for ways to resolve problems.
Feel resentful when I don't get my way.	Look for ways to put others first.

Chapter 10

"Who is the enemy?"

Preparing

Meet the McDaniel family. Lori and Linda, confident 15-year-old twin sisters, are Jim and Mary's only children. The family has only ever known military life. Both of their grandfathers and several uncles also served in the military, so being military brats was very acceptable. The girls have always had positive attitudes about all the trainings, moves and deployments which was normal life for them and their family. They have always been willing to help their mother whenever their father was away for long periods of time.

The talented girls actually loved moving and making new friends and getting involved in all sorts of activities wherever they lived. Church life was also an important part of their lives. The church they attended had a dynamic youth ministry. Because of their musical abilities to sing and play several musical instruments, they were often asked to lead the worship singing. The youth pastor was actively training the young people through accountability roles in the group such as musicians, small group leaders, and event planners, building into those who did not shirk from responsibilities and making the youth group one of the best in the city.

Because there were so many military kids in the group, the young pastor wanted to teach concepts relevant to what military families are going through but with a Biblical foundation. The topic for the month had to do with dealing with the main enemy of their lives, Satan. Many young people have not been taught how to fight this number one spiritual enemy of every human being. The girls were thrilled to be a part of the interesting and fascinating study. What they didn't know was how important it would be to them.

It was now time to get prepared for another *Welcome Home* party for the McDaniel family. Captain McDaniel had been a part of a MEU or Marine Expeditionary Unit for the last several months. The girls never really knew what their father does when he goes off to

float around the world but the latest assignment meant he'd been gone for 8 1/2 months. They were looking forward to having him back home again.

The day finally arrived. They dragged out the "welcome home" signs they'd used for several reunions, and skipping school was a plus. When they finally saw their father, they ran up to him with hugs and kisses. Mrs. McDaniel was beaming with her approval to see the girls so excited to see him. But when she looked into her husband's eyes, she saw something was different. She couldn't put her finger on it so she dismissed her notion that something was wrong.

As the weeks zoomed by with everyone's busy lives taking over, problems began to emerge which the family hadn't ever experienced before. Normally, Capt. McDaniel was a fun-loving, good-natured sort of person. But during the last few weeks every conversation had been intense. The underlying tone was impatience with everything around him. He would cuss out drivers on the road, and he would yell at his wife for silly little things almost every day. He lost patience if the girls were not ready for dinner or to go somewhere exactly when he asked them to be. More and more the girls were shying away from even wanting to be in the same room as their father.

Lori and Linda decided to make an appointment with the youth pastor at their church to see if he had any good ideas about what to do. He reminded them of the Bible study they had completed a while back about the real enemy that all human beings encounter daily. He gave them several ideas of how to talk with their father about what they'd learned. He also suggested that their father may be experiencing Post-Traumatic Stress. He said they should first be prepared with the knowledge about Combat Trauma and PTS. Secondly, he suggested they spend time praying very specific prayers for their father and the situation before having a family talk time.

10

What to learn?

First: Preparing to meet the enemy – Satan

His origin

Look up Ezekiel 28:11-19 and write down some descriptive phrases of how Satan sees himself. (The downfall of the King of Tyre is likened to Satan and his activities.)

_____

_____

_____

_____

Now describe what keeps Satan doing what he wants to do:

_____

_____

His objectives

1. Be as deceitful as possible toward all humans so he can get back at God.
2. Cause as much chaos as possible to keep humans from following God.
3. Turn humans away from God and from following Jesus Christ.
4. Use humans to stage rebellions against God with pain, wars, abuse.

His tactics

Note: Read each verse and record what you learn about Satan's way of deceiving:

Matthew 4:1

_____

_____

_____

2 Corinthians 11:14,15

_____

_____

_____

Matthew 4:8,9

_____

_____

_____

Luke 8:11,12

_____

_____

_____

Second: Preparing to see the enemy – Satan

Note: Read the list below for possible tactics of the enemy. Know that God has a plan for you to combat any of Satan's deceptive ways. Check any you have noticed in yourself or others close to you. Then ask God to remove the temptations.

James 1:5 – "If any of you lacks wisdom, let him ask God, who gives generously to all without reproach, and it will be given him."

☐ Holding on to grudges or bitterness against God and others

☐ Having a negative self-image

☐ Attempting or having thoughts of suicide

☐ Rebelling against authority

☐ Seeking or giving consent to occult powers or revelations

☐ Participating in psychic phenomena such as spells, magic, fortunetelling

☐ Rejecting what is known to be true

☐ Abusing alcohol and drugs

☐ Carrying the shock and trauma of combat to the point of despair

☐ Experiencing prolonged sleeplessness due to Combat Trauma

☐ Letting anger rule your life

☐ Participating in false religions or cults

10

Third: Preparing to fight the enemy — Satan

Note: We have been given weapons to use against Satan and his ways. Use these weapons on a regular basis so that your enemy, Satan, will see that you are not alone in fighting off his deceptions.

Weapon #1 — Our Authority

1. Read Ephesians 1:19-23 and write down what it has to say about Jesus Christ's power and authority.

_____

_____

2. What kind of power does Jesus have and over whom?

_____

_____

3. According to Colossians 2:9,10 who else has this same kind of power?

_____

_____

Weapon #2 — Our Spiritual Armor

Read Ephesians 6:13-17 and complete the following sentences using the choices found in the illustration on the next page.

1. A _____ protects us from anything launched at us from our enemy.

2. The _____ guards our heart from deceptions.

3. The _____ keeps our minds from believing anything but the truth.

4. Strapping on the _____ alerts us to the lies and deceitful tactics of the enemy.

5. We can use the _____ as both a defensive and offensive weapon against the lies of the enemy.

6. The _____ keeps us walking on the path of life without stumbling.

(Answers: 1. Shield of Faith 2. Breastplate of Righteousness 3. Helmet of Salvation 4. Belt of Truth 5. Sword of the Spirit 6. Boots of the Gospel of Peace)

Sword of
the Spirit

Breastplate
of Righteousness

Helmet of Salvation

Boots of the
Gospel of Peace

Belt of Truth

Shield of Faith

Weapon #3 – The Word of God

Note: When God created the world, He commanded matter into existence. To neutralize Satan, heal the sick, calm a storm, raise the dead, and control demons, Jesus spoke a word of command. His disciples also spoke commands and released God's power. Look at the verse on the left and write what happened as a result of the spoken Word of God in the right column.

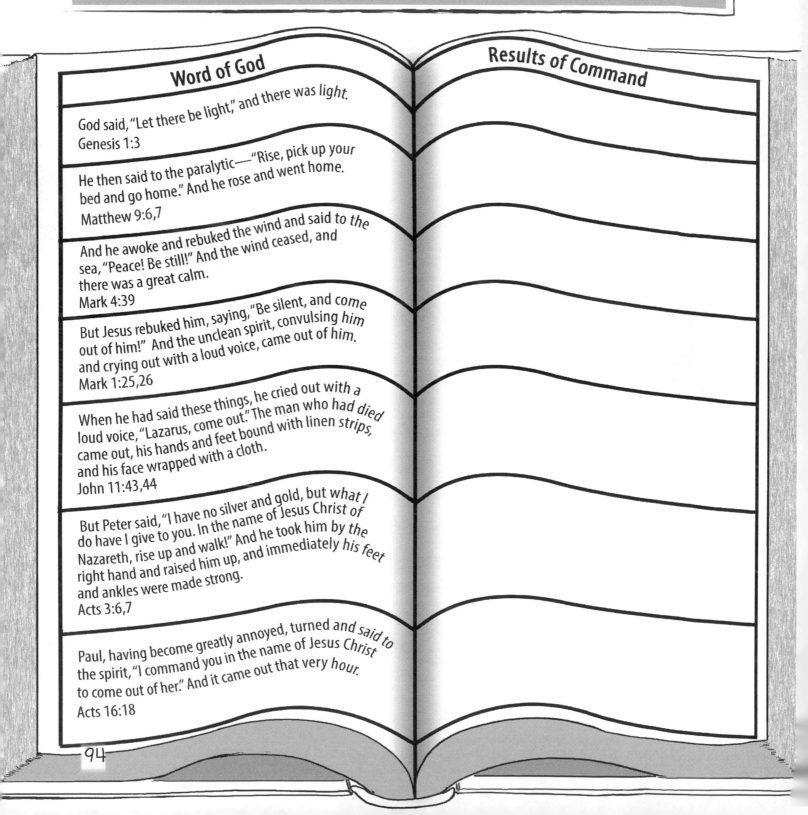

Word of God

God said, "Let there be light," and there was light.
Genesis 1:3

He then said to the paralytic—"Rise, pick up your bed and go home." And he rose and went home.
Matthew 9:6,7

And he awoke and rebuked the wind and said to the sea, "Peace! Be still!" And the wind ceased, and there was a great calm.
Mark 4:39

But Jesus rebuked him, saying, "Be silent, and come out of him!" And the unclean spirit, convulsing him and crying out with a loud voice, came out of him.
Mark 1:25,26

When he had said these things, he cried out with a loud voice, "Lazarus, come out." The man who had died came out, his hands and feet bound with linen strips, and his face wrapped with a cloth.
John 11:43,44

But Peter said, "I have no silver and gold, but what I do have I give to you. In the name of Jesus Christ of Nazareth, rise up and walk!" And he took him by the right hand and raised him up, and immediately his feet and ankles were made strong.
Acts 3:6,7

Paul, having become greatly annoyed, turned and said to the spirit, "I command you in the name of Jesus Christ to come out of her." And it came out that very hour.
Acts 16:18

Results of Command

What to ask?

Note: Answer the following questions truthfully but remember to be respectful of each other and your family members. Be a good listener. Do not share or repeat anything you hear outside the group. Confidentiality helps make the group a safe place to share from your heart. Everyone should be made to feel accepted no matter what. Everyone should feel open to sharing as this gives hope to those who speak. Sharing God's love and His Word brings encouragement and transformed lives.

Q.1 Have you ever fallen victim to the temptations of Satan? _____

What happened?

_____

_____

_____

Q.2 Are there areas of chronic defeat in your life? _____

What have you done to defeat Satan's attempts to get you away from God?

_____

_____

10

Q.3 Which one of the weapons on the previous pages do you feel the most comfortable using to combat the enemy?

_____

_____

Which of the weapons do you need more practice in using?

_____

_____

What keeps you from feeling confident in battling the lies of Satan in your life?

_____

_____

What to take away?

Note: Use God's Word to fight off temptations for yourself and for those you love by repeating the following or similar prayers. Share this knowledge with those around you who have not found victory over the sin in their lives.

Addressing God

"Dear Father, Satan is tempting me to sin against You. He wants me to do _____. But I desire to master him. Please fill me with Your Holy Spirit. I take my position seated with Christ at Your right hand in the heavenly realms above all forces of darkness. With Your blessing and protection, and in Your authority, I ask You to help me resist my enemy, and thereby defeat him. Amen"

Addressing Satan

"Satan, I address you in the name and authority of the Lord Jesus Christ, King of kings and Lord of lords, who has bought me with His blood and made me a child of the Most High God. I am aware of your attempts to cause me to sin. In doing so, you have transgressed the commandment of God, for He has said in His Word, 'You shall not _____.' You are trying to get me to commit this sin, so you are in the wrong. Therefore, by the authority given to me by God Himself, I command you to cease your activities directed at me, remove yourself from my area and go where Jesus Christ tells you to go."

Thanking God

Dear Father, Thank You for helping me see my need to reach out to You and Your Word to fight off my number one enemy. Just as you helped Jesus fight off Satan when tempted, I ask that You would minister to me and strengthen the weaknesses in my life to make me a stronger Christian. Amen"

What does God say?

Ephesians 6:12 – "For we do not wrestle against flesh and blood, but against the rulers, against the authorities, against the cosmic powers over this present darkness, against the spiritual forces of evil in the heavenly places."

We all have the power to **prepare** us to fight Satan. Ask God to show you an area you would like Him to help you with. Write down your idea, and then dig into the Word of God to find a verse that will help you fight the battle with Satan.

_____

_____

_____

_____

_____

_____

_____

_____

_____

_____

_____

10

What to pray?

"Dear Lord, Thank You for the work You did on the cross that gives me the power to resist temptation that leads to sin. Help me be a good example of someone who trusts You for the outcome in all areas of my life including my father's behavior. Please help him know how You can help him through the pain he is experiencing as a result of Combat Trauma. I pray he would find strength in You and his heart would be healed. Amen."

What's next?

Area of Need	Verse to Look Up	How will He Help?
When I am afraid	Isaiah 41:10	
When I feel alone	Psalm 139:7-11	
When I have no hope	Psalm 42:5,6a	
When I'm at the end	2 Corinthians 12:9	
When I don't know what's next	James 1:5	
When I don't feel safe	Psalm 18:30-32	
When I feel unloved	Zephaniah 3:17,18	
When God seems far away	Romans 8:38,39	
When darkness overwhelms me	1 Peter 1:6,7	
When I am worried	Matthew 6:25-34	

Chapter 11

"How can we help?"

Contributing

Meet the Adams family. The three teens, Grace, Jonathan and Ellie have been friends with the Perez kids *(Chapter 8)* ever since the last duty station where both families were at the same base in Spain. Jonathan and Tomas met their freshman year as eager students in several computer classes. Over the three years the families were in Spain, they had many BBQ dinners in their back yards and often went to local events together. They coordinated most of their leave time by renting two travel vans and spending many hours, days and weeks exploring Europe.

Now that both families were stateside, they were thrilled at again being stationed at the same base. Jonathan and Tomas had become best friends and they both loved anything to do with computers. They had each built their own personalized computers using money they earned by tutoring people in using computer software. If any question came up concerning the inner workings of computers, the guys usually had the answer or knew where to find out what they needed to know.

When Tomas decided to start a support group for military kids at the high school, *The Triple Win Club*, the first person he talked to about being in the leadership was Jonathan. In fact, the other Adams teens and his brother and sister all wanted to have a part in pioneering a successful group. They all felt there was a great need to help families affected by loved ones coming back from the war zones with Combat Trauma. Tomas gave each one some research on various topics to investigate and told them to be ready to report to everyone at their first meeting in a couple of weeks.

By the time the day for the first meeting came around, everyone was eager to share what they had learned. Tomas had made copies for everyone of the proposal he had presented to the principal *(see page 73)* and handed out a manila file folder containing those papers. Everyone had made copies of their own research notes to add to the file folders. After all the papers had been passed out, Tomas asked everyone to sit down and be ready to follow along as each shared their research results.

The supervising teacher, who had said he would love to help in any way, joined them for the meeting. He was a former Navy Captain and after serving 20 years had gone back to school to get a teaching degree in mathematics. Jonathan and Tomas felt he was the best teacher they ever had and were thrilled that he had wanted to be the group sponsor. They also had another connection with him since he was a member of the same church that both families attended. The group was excited as the first meeting began, knowing that this would change all of their lives.

What to learn?

Note: Tomas invited each of the teens in the meeting to report on what they had discovered about the topics he had assigned to them for research.

Gabriel's Report

Task: Find out how many teens there are in active duty military families..

1. Discovered a comprehensive website loaded with great information for all members of an active duty military family: www.militaryonesource.mil

2. Discovered that there are approximately 230,000 teens, ages 13-19, in the 1.8 million children in active duty military families of all branches.

Rachel's Report

Task: Find information on how many military families there are in the local high schools.

1. Discovered there are seven high schools in the area where teens from active duty families go to school. (Still working on getting the numbers from each of the schools.)

2. Discovered many of the schools have active Jr. ROTC (Junior Reserve Officers' Training Corps) programs for students interested in going into the military after graduation.

Jonathan's Report

Task: Design social media accounts for *The Triple Win Club.*

1. Designed a logo and gave a report on all the accounts established for FaceBook, Twitter, and InstaGram.

2. Used <u>surveymonkey.com</u> to design a ten-question survey, linking it on Facebook, for military kids in the local high schools. He will tabulate the results for the next meeting.

3. Designed a survey for the parents of military kids but is waiting for more input from the leadership committee before implementing it.

Ellie's Report

Task: Recruit others who want to help, including students and parents.

1. Contacted other military friends and their parents to begin making a database of those willing to help in some way.

2. Reported on a local printer who had served in the military and wants to be available for printing fliers, posters or whatever is needed.

3. Presented their needs to the local Christian Women's Fellowship on base.

What to ask?

 Q.1 What are some ways to reach out to the military teens in the high schools?

_____

_____

 Q.2 What activities can *The Triple Win Club* do to bring unity and awareness to the community of the needs of the military kids in our midst?

_____

_____

 Q.3 What types of appreciation events can we provide to show our thankfulness for military teens as they adjust to the military life they lead?

_____

_____

What to take away?

> Note: One of the first brainstorming sessions for the teens resulted in the following list of ideas on how to be a positive influence while a family member heals from potential Combat Trauma. There could be many more ideas of how to help during the healing process. Each family's situation will be different. It is best to be creative in how to adapt the suggestions for each situation.

Military teens' support ideas when parents may have Combat Trauma

- Be committed and supportive for the whole family, no matter what.

- Show extra love and patience for younger brothers and sisters.

- Be willing to put some activities aside in order to be a driver for appointments or to pick up kids from school.

- Be informed about what PTSD/TBI does to the person suffering from it.

- Read about conflict resolution ahead of time to prevent fights.

- Be someone who shows respect, kindness and consideration.

- Be anxious for nothing; trust everything to God in prayer (Philippians 4:6,7).

- Be intentional on having good conversations with the family members.

- Be willing to forgive unusual behavior such as emotional outbursts.

- Be encouraging and accepting especially when uncertainty appears.

- Be proactive in showing an extra amount of understanding and love.

- Be someone who seeks spiritual help from the Bible, prayer and fellowship with like-minded friends.

Add your own ideas to the list of how to show a positive attitude:

_____

_____

_____

_____

11

What does God say?

Luke 6:38 — "Give, and it will be given to you. Good measure, pressed down, shaken together, running over, will be put into your lap. For with the measure you use it will be measured back to you."

Look for ways to **contribute** to the healing process from Combat Trauma. **Be available** without resentment. **Be willing** without attitude. **Be loving** even when it hurts, for God is at work in your life too. He knows how much you are trying to make a difference whether it is in a support role for a fellow teen or as a teen with a family that knows Combat Trauma issues.

What to pray?

"Dear Lord, thank You for all the help You are to me and my family. Help me be a shining light to all those around me. Give me words to say, a serving heart and a readiness to put others before myself. Heal my loved one back to complete health in body, mind and soul. Thank You for the ideas You give us as we think of how to support those who could use a friend. Amen."

What's next?

Contributing through prayer

Note: *The Triple Win Club* leadership team gave each member some Bible verses. Using those verses as examples, they were to write a prayer concerning their family dynamics. Try it yourself. *(More verses are in the Appendix on page 127.)*

Verse Reference	Sample Prayer	Your Prayer
Philippians 4:6,7	"Lord, help me not to be anxious about my dad's anger. Help me to see You can guard my heart and mind and feel Jesus' love for me."	
1 John 5:14,15	"Lord, I can have confidence in knowing You will help my mom with her depression. It is You I trust."	
Ephesians 1:17-21	"Lord, help my dad's heart know You and the hope of Your calling. Help him seek You and Your power."	
Ephesians 3:14-19	"Lord, help us all to be strengthened by the power of the Holy Spirit and may Christ dwell in our hearts."	
Colossians 1:9-12	"Lord, we ask for the filling of the knowledge of Your will in all spiritual wisdom and understanding for each of our lives."	
1 Chronicles 4:10	"Lord, I ask for You to bless my dad and mom. Keep them from harm and pain."	

11

Chapter 12

Meet the Henning family. It has been two months since Master Sergeant Henning returned from his latest deployment. Mrs. Henning has readily accepted the roles of both mother and father duties each time he's been gone and for the most part, it has gone smoothly. Madison, who is the oldest of the four children, is in her second year at the local community college. She is just shy of one class before transferring over to a four year university. She is studying to be a social worker and has already been accepted at the school of her choice. She has a goal of staying in school to go for her MSW or Master of Social Work as soon as she finishes her bachelor's degree.

The youngest in the family are twins, Ben and Emma. They are 13 and are looking forward to entering high school next school year. Both are very involved in sports, playing tennis and soccer. They are also best friends and popular wherever they go to school because of their positive attitudes in life and work ethic as students. The shelves in their rooms are lined with trophies for all kinds of accomplishments in athletics as well as in academics. They both have ambitious goals of applying for scholarships when they enter university to study sports medicine.

>>>>>>>>>>>>>>>>>>>>>>>>>>

But Carl, the 15-year-old middle child, has always struggled in the family dynamics. You could look at his position in the family as the reason he had so much difficulty, or the frequent long absences of his father as another factor. And also look at his academic records each year because though he has always tried to get the grades his siblings receive, he has never measured up. One area he does excel in is skateboarding and he takes every opportunity to hang out at the local skateboard park. Because of the busy schedules of the whole family, Carl's mom often takes him to the park but then has to rush somewhere to drop off or pick up one of the twins. It has been a challenge for her to be able to stay and watch.

Ever since returning from the latest overseas assignment, MSGT Henning has had his own difficulties. The other day, just as Carl came through the front door, the wind blew it closed with a loud bang. His father jumped up from reading the newspaper and got nose to nose with his son. He had never yelled at him as loud as he did that day, without even trying to find out the fact that the wind had blown the door shut before Carl could stop it. Carl seemed to be unable to please his father, no matter what he did and he began to resent the negative focus put on him. He's taken the brunt of his father's short temper more frequently since the last deployment. The latest reason for yelling at him was an average report card. Carl ran to his room and slammed the door shut to get away from his father.

Carl's mom decided it was time to intervene so she took her husband outside to sit under the patio awning, where she could calm him down so they could talk in private. She, too, had growing concerns with the way her husband had been acting. Something must be going on. She felt compelled to confront him to try to find out if this attitude of his was going to be the new normal or if they were ever going to see the old way he interacted with his family before his deployment. Knowing how sensitive Carl was to the academic differences between him and his siblings, she did not want him to be ostracized by his father any longer. Her husband needed to realize that he should be coming alongside Carl and helping him, not always putting him down. She wondered how he was going to react to her insights.

12

What to learn?

Dad's triggers	Dad's reactions	How to pray for God's help
An argument	Can push the anger to maximum	**Pray for peace** *Philippians 4:6,7*
News reports on war	Brings back vivid memories	**Pray for strength** *Psalm 28:7*
Movie with violence	Brings feelings of vulnerability	**Pray for rest** *Psalm 16:7-9,11*
Seeing a car accident	Makes the heart pound harder	**Pray for security** *Romans 8:38,39*
Certain smells	Reminder of war zone	**Pray for faith** *1 Peter 1:6,7*
Bad relationship	Brings loss of interest in people	**Pray for God's love** *Zephaniah 3:17,18*
Holidays	Reminder of lonely times or the loss of friends	**Pray for comfort** *2 Thessalonians 2:16,17*
Loud Noises	Startles because it sounds like gun fire	**Pray for calmness** *Psalm 62:8*
Disappointment	Brings a feeling of hopelessness	**Pray for hope** *Psalm 143:4-8*

Note: Carl's mom suggested that their family have a Family Talk Time. She wanted everyone to contribute discussion questions, including MSGT Henning. The list you see below is a copy of the questions everyone in the family brought to the table for discussion. Knowing every family has their own set of dynamics, write out questions you have in your mind, especially if you don't see your questions on the list below.

The Henning Family Talk Time Questions

- What kind of activities can we all do together as a family?

- What makes you feel happy?

- What makes you feel sad?

- What surprised you the most after Dad/you returned home?

- What forms of communication while Dad was gone did you like the best? Why?

- What kinds of activities do you like to do the most when not at work or school?

- What was the hardest day for you while Dad was gone?

- What surprised you the most during this last deployment?

- What is something which annoys you the most?

- Why are you acting differently than before you left?

- What happened while you were away at war?

- What is one thing you wish would change in our family?

- What did you think about God while you were gone? While Dad was gone?

- What is something you wish would happen in the future?

- What is one thing you wish others would know about you?

What questions would you want to ask in your family's Talk Time?

_____

_____

_____

_____

12

What to ask?

 Q.1 Do you have a better understanding about how PTSD/Combat Trauma affects someone suffering? _____ What do you still want to know?

_____

_____

_____

 Q.2 Share with the group what changes you will make in attitude, behavior or body language around the person in your family who has PTSD symptoms?

_____

_____

_____

 Q.3 Do you relate to any of the teens in the Henning family? _____ Have you ever felt neglected in your family?

_____

_____

What I wish others knew about military teens

- We want to be recognized for serving too.
- We want you to know we readily take on responsibilities while a parent serves overseas.
- We have a story to tell of sacrifice, adaptability and transition skills.
- We love the friends we have made all over the world.
- We want lasting friendships even though we move around a lot.
- We understand what it means to serve and are proud of our parent's service.
- We want teachers to be understanding when we change schools a lot.
- We hope more people praise my father for his career choice.
- We have learned to juggle many activities because of added responsibilities.
- We have a lot to share about other cultures and people groups where we have lived.

Now it is your turn. Write down and share other points you wish others knew about you as a military teen.

_____

_____

_____

_____

_____

_____

_____

What does God say?

1 Peter 4:10 – "As each has received a gift, use it to serve one another, as good stewards of God's varied grace."

Instead of having a negative reaction to someone you love because of PTSD symptoms, take on the job of caring and compassion. See how you as a family can **seek God's help** for every step on the way to complete healing for all.

Do you see this as a possibility happening in your family? _____ Why or why not?

_____

_____

_____

12

What to pray?

"Lord, may we be a family that turns to You every day for guidance while we help
_____ see complete healing. Restore our hearts to trust You with
great and mighty results. We desire to be an example to those around us of how
much we love You and want everyone to understand Your ways. Help us call upon You
for everything that comes our way. Amen."

What's next?

Note: After speaking to her husband, Mrs. Henning decided to ask for help in dealing with the issues her family was experiencing. She and the twins had purposed to keep extra busy and were ignoring the negative attitude. Mrs. Henning found help online and also from friends she had in the small group study she attended at their church. Listed below in the chart are some of the suggestions.

Working toward a healthy home life for a military family

What NOT to do	What to do
Yell or be aggressive toward one child in the family more than the others **... causes anxiety**	Reach out to show affection toward all the children in the family **... brings security**
Share graphic details of combat with family members **... causes stress**	Explain how the war zone made you feel without telling details **... brings understanding**
Isolation from the outside world by the Combat Trauma sufferer **... causes confusion**	Realize what causes triggers and inform family members **... brings compassion**
Show disinterest in accomplishments of children in the home **... causes insecurity**	Encourage each teenager for their individual work at school **... brings good self-worth**
Ignore unusual reactions to small incidents not worthy of drama **... causes distress**	Address drama calmly and point out a better behavior reaction **... brings peace**
Make excuses for hurtful behavior made by the Combat Trauma sufferer **... causes disrespect**	Create an atmosphere of openness so all see the good resolutions **... brings maturity**
Lie to cover up an embarrassing situation **... causes bad learned behavior**	Provide honest answers and information for questions asked **... brings reassurance and love**

Chapter 13

Meet the Chase family. A whirlwind of events had been stressing out every member of the family ever since Lieutenant Colonel Chase was medically discharged from his military career. No one saw it coming and each member had been dealing with the major injuries as a result of a land mine explosion he had endured on his last deployment assignment. After a long recovery, physical therapy, and piles of paperwork, the date had finally arrived. He had been retired. The unit he was in put on a wonderful program to honor his years of outstanding service and making the ultimate sacrifice of losing both legs from the knees down. The whole Chase family was present including his parents and several siblings. It was a bittersweet day, laden with sadness and celebration at the same time.

Alex, who was 17 years old, respected his father so much. He looked forward to his own high school graduation so he could make the pledge to become a part of the military tradition of service by his father, uncles, grandfathers and cousins. You could say this was a multi-generational military family and they were so proud of the tradition. Alex's sister and brother, Aria, 15, and Aiden, 13, had taken their father's catastrophic injuries the hardest of everyone. None of their relatives who had served or were still serving had ever been injured. They wondered what life would hold for them now that their father would begin living back at home full-time.

It has now been several months since the retirement party. Life for the Chase family has been turned upside down. Because of the nature of the devastating injuries resulting from an IED explosion, LTC Chase has been accepted into a special program that assists the wounded and their families through recovery, treatment and rehabilitation. Their family has been adopted by a Buddy Family who is taking every member under their wing and is helping them through the process of healing. The families are matched with similar interests and ages of the children.

During the many surgeries and recovery time necessary for their father's legs to heal before being fitted with prosthetics, Alex and his brother and sister had instant friends whenever they were able to visit their father. It was only a six hour drive from their home; so during long weekends and all holidays the Chase family was together with their Buddy Family. The extra support and friendship made the transition from being an active duty officer on the field to being a full-time recovering wounded warrior much more tolerable. LTC Chase's family went from feeling overwhelmed to increasing confidence about the future, whatever that may be. It was truly a blessing to have someone to talk with about their feelings and to help think of ways to cope with the situation on a daily basis.

Aria and Aiden were especially encouraged by the additional education they received about the injuries both physical and psychological which they knew their father was experiencing. It gave them hope to know complete healing would come in time and the new normal for the family life in the Chase household would be one they could all handle. Whenever the family was in town for a visit, they always enjoyed going to church with their Buddy Family. A whole new world opened up to them once they learned to have God involved in the healing for their whole family. Mrs. Chase saw a new attitude of hope in each of her teens that seemed to erase the stress that had been there for months. She began a search near her home of a church similar to the one her children loved to attend whenever they visited their father. There was so much more hope in her heart then she had ever felt since life had taken a turn for the worse because of her husband's injuries.

13

What to learn?

Characteristics of a good buddy family/teen/friend

1. **Reliable** – Show a caring attitude that never wavers.
2. **Strong** – Show strength in helping to carry the burdens.
3. **Gentle** – Show understanding when encountering emotions.
4. **Kind** – Show an extra measure of compassion when needed.
5. **Patient** – Show grace when needed.
6. **Love** – Show consistent acceptance, no matter what.
7. **Giving** – Show a heart that loves to bless others.
8. **Intentional** – Show initiative in creating truthful encounters.
9. **Respectful** – Show ways to give encouraging remarks.
10. **Supportive** – Show a positive and balanced friendship.

Using the Chase family as a case study, discuss ways you could show each of the characteristics listed above while interacting with each member of the family. Think of practical ways to reach out to them to show you care.

Characteristic	Your Idea
Reliable	
Strong	
Gentle	
Kind	
Patient	
Love	
Giving	
Intentional	
Respectful	
Supportive	

What to ask?

 Q.1 Do you feel you have an understanding about how Combat Trauma affects the wounded? _____ Affects the family? _____ What are your questions?

_____

_____

_____

13

 Q.2 What does it mean to be a confidential buddy?

_____

_____

_____

 Q.3 If you are a teen in a family where Combat Trauma affects a loved one, what do you want others to know about what you are experiencing?

_____

_____

_____

What to take away?

Looking for a church

Note: Mrs. Chase and her teens decided to take on the task of finding a church they would all love. She asked their Buddy Family for advice on how to look for a healthy church. The following is a list they used in their search:

A healthy church

Characteristic	Biblical Foundation	Yes or No
Teaching from God's Word	Psalm 119:9-12	
Balanced worship for all ages	Psalm 138:1-4	
Lift up Jesus Christ as Lord	Philippians 3:7-11	
Importance of heartfelt prayer	John 15:7	
Actively training disciples	Matthew 28:18-20	
Caring for and loving others	Mark 12:28-31	
Actively developing leaders	Ephesians 4:11-13	
Intentional outreach and missions	Acts 13:1-3	
Actively empower vision to grow	Colossians 1:5,6	
Honor true stewardship	Proverbs 3:9,10	
Appropriate programming for all	Philippians 3:12-14	
Open to replicating church	Acts 1:8	

What other thoughts or questions do you have about finding a healthy church?

_____

_____

_____

_____

What does God say?

*Jeremiah 29:11 – "For I know the **plans** I have for you, declares the Lord, **plans** for welfare and not for evil, to give you a **future** and a **hope**."*

God is very aware of the dreams you have for your family. He wants you to have a **future** filled with love, joy, peace, patience, kindness, goodness, faithfulness, gentleness and self-control. Do you believe this is possible? _____ Why or why not?

_____

_____

_____

_____

_____

What to pray?

"Lord, we need Your help in so many areas. Most of all we ask for a complete healing for our family physically, emotionally, and spiritually. Guide us to the church where we can learn about the hope You want us to have. We want to reach out to You more for we do not have the strength to do this alone. Thank You for those You put into our lives to encourage and bless us. We love what You are doing to guide us through this drastic change. We love You! Amen."

13

What's next?

Working together as a family team

Step One - Prayer Guidance

- Be consistent in praying for each member of the family and their needs.

- Encourage one another in positive ways; be intentional.

- Post daily prayer requests on a white board for family to know how to pray.

Step Two - Educational Guidance

- Be informed about the next steps for the treatments for the one wounded.

- Use a Year Calendar poster to list important dates for each person.

- Talk through how each one feels about the possibility of moving.

Step Three - Logistical Guidance

- Research the types of jobs LTC Chase could do based on his abilities, likes and passions.

- Research the types of training LTC Chase could take in order to qualify for a job regardless of his disability.

- Brainstorm the ideal places in the country where each would like to live and go to school.

Step Four - Spiritual Guidance

- Obtain a Bible journal for each member of the family.

- Make plans to study the same books of the Bible using the following method. The book of John is a good place to start. Write down your thoughts and observations according to SPACE-Q..

  S - Sins to confess
  P - Promises to claim
  A - Actions to avoid
  C - Commands to obey
  E - Examples to follow
  Q - Questions I need answered

Example:

John 1:1-13

• S: --

• P: God made all things. Jesus made all things

• A: Thank God for his power and might.

• C: --

• E: Jesus was the light of the world... help me be a light

• Q: What am I hiding in the darknes that should be in the light?

13

Additional Resources

A Catholic Teen's Guide to Tough Stuff: Straight Talk, Real Issues by Jim Auer [Liguori Publications, 2003]

Battlefield of the Mind for Teens by Joyce Meyer, Todd Hafer [Faithwords, 2006]

Connecting with God by Chris Adsit [Disciplemakers International, 2001]

Daily Reflections by Highly Effective Teens by Sean Covey [Simon & Schuster, 1999]

Discovering Your Identity in Christ by Charles Stanley [Thomas Nelson, 1999]

Don't Let Your Emotions Run Your Life for Teens by Sheri Van Dijk MSW [Childswork/Childsplay, 2011]

Down Range: To Iraq and Back by Bridget C. Cantrell, PhD and Chuck Dean [WordSmith Publishing, 2005]

Finding My Way: A Teen's Guide to Living with a Parent Who Has Experienced Trauma by Michelle D. Sherman, PhD. & DeAnne M. Sherman [Seeds of Hope Books, 2005]

Have You Made the Wonderful Discovery of the Spirit-Filled Life? booklet written by Bill Bright. Copyright 1966, 1995. New Life Publications, a ministry of Campus Crusade for Christ. Available at www.crustore.org. Described in Chapter 7.

Learning How to Trust...Again by Dr. Ed Delph and Alan & Pauly Heller [Destiny Image, 2007]

The Case for Faith: Student Edition by Lee Strobel with Jane Vogel [Zondervan/Youth Specialties, 2010]

The Case for Grace: Student Edition by Lee Strobel with Jane Vogel [Zondervan, 2015]

The PTSD Workbook for Teens by Libbi Palmer, PSYD [Childswork/Childsplay, 2012]

The 7 Habits of Highly Effective Teens by Sean Covey [Franklin Covey, 1999]

The 6 Most Important Decisions You'll Ever Make: Personal Workbook by Sean Covey [Franklin Covey, 2009]

Things I've Learned Lately by Danae Jacobson [Multnomah Books, 2010]

Turn My Mourning Into Dancing: Finding Hope in Hard Times by Henri Nouwen [Word Publishing/Thomas Nelson, 2001]

When God Doesn't Make Sense by James C. Dobson [Living Books, 2011]

When You Can't Say "I Forgive You" by Grace Ketterman & Duvid Hazard [NavPress, 2000]

Where is God When it Hurts? By Philip Yancey [Harper Collins, 1977]

Wild at Heart: Discovering the Secret of a Man's Soul by John Eldredge [Thomas Nelson, 2001]

Appendix

The Williams family have already been through four deployments. On page 8, they used the checklist below to help them prepare for their dad's homecoming. What might your "Homecoming Checklist" look like?

Homecoming Checklist

- ☐ Mow the lawn, trim bushes and plant nice looking flowers, in season.
- ☐ Clean garage.
- ☐ Vacuum and clean carpets.
- ☐ Dust furniture, put away all unnecessary stuff sitting around.
- ☐ Bake favorite cookies or dessert.
- ☐ Plan a favorite meal and have it ready to eat when everyone is home.
- ☐ Design and make a super "Welcome Home" sign.
- ☐ Don't plan a lot of activities until we have a chance to talk it over with Dad.
- ☐ Stock the pantry with healthy snacks and drinks.
- ☐ Plan a fun talent show each member of the family have a part of, such as a Reader's Theater, acting out favorite book, or singing or playing musical instruments. Plan it well in advance so there is time for everyone to practice.
- ☐ Organize an art show with school work or art projects we did while Dad was gone.
- ☐ Be patient and not demanding of Dad's attention.

_____

_____

_____

_____

_____

More questions for
the Family Sit-Down Talk Guide

On page 41, the Johnson family used a questionnaire to prepare for their Family Sit-Down Talk. Here are some additional questions they could have used. What other questions can you think of?

1. What is a way family members can better understand what they can do when you feel sad?

2. How many times a month would you like to have a Family Talk Time?

3. When we have a monthly Family Fun Date with each member taking a turn choosing, what kinds of activities would you like to do?

4. What is one way you would love to be surprised?

_____

_____

_____

_____

More verses for prayer

On page 105, *The Triple Win Club* used a number of verses as examples for prayer concerning their family dynamics. Here are additional verses you can look up:

- Nehemiah 8:10
- Psalm 23:1
- Psalm 103:3
- Isaiah 58:8
- Isaiah 61:1
- Jeremiah 1:12
- Matthew 16:18

- Romans 12:1
- 2 Corinthians 10:5
- Ephesians 6:14-17
- Philippians 4:13
- Philippians 4:19
- 1 Peter 5:7
- 3 John 2

Index

Families

Web sites

Made in the USA
San Bernardino, CA
30 July 2020